Coming down
the Zambezi

By the same author

Baleia, Baleia

Coming down
the Zambezi

Bernard Venables

THE TRAVEL BOOK CLUB
LONDON: 1976

The Travel Book Club
125 Charing Cross Road
London, WC2H 0EB

To Kufekisa (Kay) Sifuniso

Printed and bound in Great Britain by
REDWOOD BURN LIMITED
Trowbridge & Esher

Illustrations

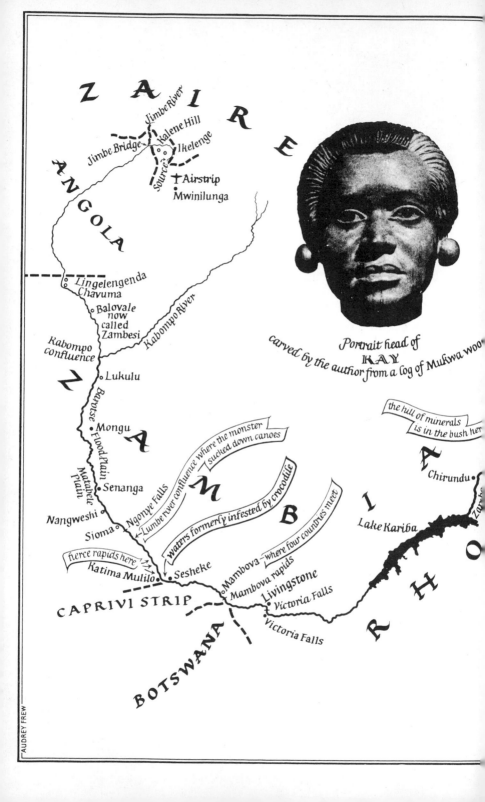

ZAIRE

ANGOLA

Jimbe River

Jimbe Bridge

Kalene Hill

Ikelenge

Source

Airstrip

Mwinilunga

Lingelengenda

Chavuma

Balovale
now
called
Zambesi

Kabompo River

Kabompo
confluence

ZAMBIA

Lukulu

Barotse

Mongu

Flood Plain

Ngonye Falls

Lumbe river confluence where the monster
sucked down canoes

the hill of minerals
is in the bush here

Chirundu

Matabele
Plain

Senanga

waters formerly infested by crocodile

Lake Kariba

Nangweshi

Sioma

fierce rapids here

Mambova — where four countries meet

Katima Mulilo

Sesheke

Mambova rapids

Livingstone

Victoria Falls

CAPRIVI STRIP

BOTSWANA

Victoria Falls

RHO

Zaze

Portrait head of
KAY
carved by the author from a log of Mukwa wood

AUDREY FREW

Coming down the Zambezi

Journey's end

Feira

Mpata Gorge

...lley

MOZAMBIQUE

DESIA

0 Scale of 50 miles 100

INDIAN OCEAN

Acknowledgement

Such description of tribal rituals and beliefs as this book contains were, in the first case, the outcome of first-hand but random observation and experience. But, because it was so unco-ordinated, without enough pattern to make it intelligible, I subsequently consulted various authorities. Of those I must acknowledge particularly V. W. Turner whose book, *The Drums of Affliction* (Oxford), makes absorbing reading for anyone who wants to know more of the mysticism of the Ndembu people of the Zambezi's source country.

I

The last few yards were down a steep fall of stony track, out of sun into cavernous shade. Smooth boles soared to the rain forest canopy; sunny dazzle tangled the openings in the canopy and fuzzes of sun hung among the boughs. A host of yellow butter-flies drifted like motes. It was still early in the day and it felt cool.

One tree had aerial roots, an inverted candelabrum, and it was under them that the water started. Within the roots there was a tiny brown pool, twelve inches across. From there the water ran on, a rivulet feeling down between the dense carpet of leathery dead brown leaves on either bank. *That* then was the beginning. I crouched and drank the water with a sense of ceremony. Prob-ably this first runnel set me thinking of destinies because the river has great symbolism for Zambia, itself so young as an independent nation. The sense of beginning, birth, was enhanced by the secrecy and the remoteness of the forest, nearly in the very centre of Central Africa and the last extremity of Zambia. This was only fifty yards from the Congo frontier. Half a mile away, over the frontier, rises one of the sources of the great Congo river —a solemn enough thought itself.

Already in those first few feet of the river, there was teeming life. Metallic beetles skated the surface, lizards darted from my feet, into the water; little frogs straddled the current. And, already a foot from the source, there were fish, a few inches long. It was silent but with sudden and separate sounds within the silence—a bell-like call of a bird, rustlings, all sorts of minor sounds and presences under the silence.

I thought of how this had begun. I had seen the Zambezi before, far down its course at Katima Mulilo and Sesheke, and it flows magnificently there between remote banks. I had seen its mile and a quarter of width drop over the Victoria Falls. I had wondered then what sort of a beginning such a river could have. It was hard to conjecture. The feeling grew, became compulsive, that I must go to it—wherever it rose, in whatever wilderness. I would find it and follow it, for the whole of its course through Zambia.

This was the reality, an urgent little stream in the rain forest against the Congo. There were three of us and we were silent, two of us awed into silence. The third, who was our guide, was silent because we were strangers and he was shy. He had no awe for the little river; he had known that all his life and had never seen its far-away hugeness. Kay—whose name, so much more beautifully, was really Kufekisa—had been born by the river too, but at Mongu, far from there on the Barotse Plain, and there the Zambezi is a great river. She was black and I was white, but I think she was hardly less of a stranger there. Her awe was no less.

We started to walk, and again with a little solemnity. These were the first steps of a long journey. So it was for Kay and for me. Our guide was concerned only to lead us that day to his own village, Ikelengi.

Those first steps were difficult, snared and tripping. The little river was entangled in the forest. Great tree boles baulked it, and us, into twists and turns; hanging loops of liana snared our necks and arms. Sometimes the mesh of vine and scrub choked the bank so utterly that we had to step to the other bank for slightly clearer way.

'You,' I said to myself, 'are *stepping* over the Zambezi.'

The river began to grow. Almost at once it became a frontier—on the one side Zambia, on the other the Congo. It became too wide for stepping. When the leathery tangle halted us we had to leap—leap the Zambezi, out of Zambia, into the Congo. Then soon leap again, back into Zambia. Within the first mile the first tributary came in, a rivulet running its whole course from source to main river in twenty yards. The first falls came, pygmy spills, and the first infant cataracts. I remembered the huge white swirls of the cataracts near Katima Mulilo.

The sound of the water was clear in the forest—that and the bell-like bird defined the silence. The crush of our feet in the dry pile of leaves was intrusive, and I wondered when and what feet before ours had trodden there. None for a long time. The growth was so dense that no one could have passed recently and left no sign of passage.

Then, several miles from the source, the river was enlarging, taking in miniature the proper structure of a river, rapids, falls, pools, streams, glides. The pools were duskily limpid in the forest's shade, five feet across and not much less deep. To cross now we had to find a fallen bough or bole for a precarious bridge, or, with stride, leap and staggering clutch, use chance mid-stream footholds.

We went very slowly now, threading and thrusting in the thickening mesh of growth, and I was grateful to be lean. Only the spare could slink a way. Kay, five feet and perhaps a bit, was a black wisp. The guide seemed able to dis-articulate himself. For possibly two miles more we struggled, creeping under, climbing over, crossing and re-crossing the river. I thought it was becoming impossible, but because the others still seemed willing and able I must strive as best I could.

Then the guide stopped and was apologetic. He knew, he said, that I wanted to go by the river, but it was hard to go forward now. Perhaps we should move out of the forest. We made a last crossing of the river, teetering across a fallen sag of bough and vine, into the Congo.

He led us, filing through and rising a little from the river, with the trees thinning but with crowns still dense. Then the ground rose sharply; we climbed out of the aisles of the forest. Suddenly we were in a white blaze of sun. We came out from under the trees, passing abruptly from twilight into an incandescent percussion of life.

It was mid-morning; the sun was vertical. The torrent of light poured into everything, piercing the shadows and flooding the spaces between. Cicadas shrilled incessantly; the air swam with light and heat.

This was open bush, loosely forested, rather glade-like. Dead trees, bone-white and lean, reaching like arrested gestures, were reminders in the thrum of life that it is life itself which is continuous, not its units. Of the million million lives beating in the sun all were prey or predators, all part of the endless rhythm of birth and life, of death and decay, of devouring and succumbing and rebirth. So the rotation of life goes in an English meadow, but subdued, apparently tranquil, not bitten into such definition.

Yellow-billed kites wheeled above the trees, so near, so slowly floating that I could see the searching turn of their amber eyes. Praying mantises, deadly patient, awaited prey with queer mimicry of leaf and stem.

The premature coming of the rainy season, then, in October, had brought a gush of growth. Spears of grass had thrust from the crumbled red soil, flowers had sprung, butterflies dawdled among the blossoms. Life was surging—creatures hatching, creatures dying, trees fruiting, butterflies sipping, hawks stooping, insects shrilling, all life beating in the sun. The rains were early, not yet fully into their stride, but anyway, the rainy season in Central Africa does not come with a depression of steady rain. Recurrent storms rage briefly and pass, then the sun comes again, blinding-bright in the cleared air. Now the heat was augmenting, already well past the hundredth degree.

Though, down-river, no really valid picture of the source country could be imagined, I had expected that it would be some sort of ultimate forest wilderness in the hot heart of Africa, and so it was. It was apparently illimitable jungle, with no way distinguishable from another, apart from the pointer of the river forest below. It looked archaic, with the red and iron hard termite hills crowded among the trees, They looked dead. But if you break them they are intricate inside, with a million galleries and chambers; each is a metropolis. To the horde of their inhabitants, a quarter of an inch long, I suppose the next termite hill is as far and foreign as another city.

By any stem or stone there was some pygmy throng of life, each feeling itself to be a world. I saw the span of sky and bush, enormous by my scale, but relatively as infinitesimal. Under each tread of my foot there were worlds too small for seeing, all part of the same interdependence.

But for all the pulse of life there was an absence. Nothing broke from cover. There was no evidence of larger life—no antelope, no game. There were unseen things as always, snakes, smaller creatures, that will stay still in their camouflage or retreat if they can—you can be within feet of snakes and not see them. For all the stories, they are inoffensive if allowed to be. But there were no signs of game, no distant sightings, no spoor, no droppings. In these we had a practical interest.

We had to eat. The larger villages and the towns when come upon have stores and in those you can buy canned foods. It is a narrow diet and taken steadily, it palls; it is also heavy and bulky to carry. To eat reasonably and regularly you must hunt. We seemed likely to fast.

There are standbys for eating in the bush and the chief one is the guinea fowl, a substantial bird. It wanders in quite large companies and is usually ubiquitous. So I had formerly found it to be. This was country that should have an abundance. I peered ahead at

15

every open space. Guinea fowl linger in such places, avoiding ambush. There was no sight of them.

My hope had been for a wart hog which, though not a lovely animal, is very good meat, like good pork. But none was there—we saw none, nor their easily recognizable tracks. Not them nor anything else, not even the little duiker, though traditionally this is duiker country. Had too-heavy hunting been the cause, I asked the guide? It had, he said, though the patient hunter will find the duiker still.

No game for us then. But bush wandering induces an acceptance of come-what-may. The current minute is the reality. We had eaten yesterday. At Ikelengi that night we would eat again. We had some cans. But we still went circumspectly, doubling not only for density of bush but for hope of surprising at least guinea fowl. With now no sight of the river forest, I lost all sense of direction. It was hot about midday; the sun's blaze pressed. Sweat curtained our faces, saturated us. We were thirsty.

Probably our guide knew the tree. When we reached it he spread his hands, smiled widely, waved us to it in the manner of a host. Over the twist of its bare boughs its dense canopy was heavy with fruit; fruit littered the ground, small round plums, yellow and ruddy-red. I suppose they were not very good plums, rather fibrous round the stones and not very juicy. But fruits of Eden could have provided no greater refreshment. They were sweetish with a sharp tang. We ate them feverishly, spitting stones and snatching more. *Umfumu*, our guide said, was the tree's name.

Fruit, if you are sweat-drained and hungry, is wonderfully restorative. We walked on strongly although now, early afternoon, it was furnace-hot, 106 degrees (however you become adjusted to heat). It must have been two or three hours and a few miles later that, coming out of the Congo, back into Zambia, we emerged where we had started, at the commemorative stone. George and his pick-up were waiting there.

The stone stands in an open place where the track drops down into the forest where the source is. It bears a plaque, and on that an inscription.

This stone was unveiled
on 24th October 1964
to mark the attainment of Independence
after seventy years of colonial rule
and is dedicated
to all those men and women
who by personal sacrifice
enabled Independence to be achieved.
This monument stands
at the source of the Zambezi River
from which Zambia derives its Name
and which, with its great tributaries,
has played so large a part
in the life and history of its people
and commemorates
the birth of a new nation
in which all people are born free, equal
and united

George and his pick-up were there because a bush track comes there. We had gained George and the pick-up at the Boma at Mwinilunga. It had seemed fortunate at the time.

We had come in a light aircraft from Lusaka to Mwinilunga, expecting to be met at the airstrip. No one was there, nothing in the white-hot emptiness but the wheeling kites and a distant eagle. We waited for an hour, watching the lizards and listening for distant sound of a Land Rover. Then we dumped our gear in the shade of the aircraft and set out to walk the seven miles into town.

We left the sun-seared airstrip, crossed a grassy plain, and came to a village. We did not see it till we were in it because it was submerged in succulence. Much of the Central Africa that I had known is arid except in the rainy season, savannah, flat-topped thorn trees and high yellow-white grass. This was luscious, very 'tropical' as the word is usually understood. Heavy-topped evergreen trees stood over the village and, under them, stumpy palms with fronds nearly to the ground. The huts straggled through thickets of suede-textured shrubs, sags of blossom and fat banana clumps. For a mile or more the village rambled on, placidly haphazard, as if its makers had been too soaked with sun and fruitfulness ever to have bothered with a plan.

The huts were good, not made with poles, mud-filled, in the common way, but square and solid with sun-baked bricks. There was a church in the same manner, about ten feet by twenty feet, earth-floored with rough wooden benches and unglazed openings at either end for windows. The children came to us as we walked, chattering and laughing and nearly naked, with skins like purple plums with the bloom on them.

Beyond the huts there were pineapple gardens, plots of dark rich earth.

Then we left the village and came to the dirt road that goes to Mwinilunga. There we were met by a Land Rover. Because we had buzzed the town before landing local officials had come to find us. They were courteous men, grave and friendly. They took us into Mwinilunga and to the Boma to meet the District Secretary—the Boma is the administrative centre of a district, and the District Secretary is the district's administrator. This district, the Mwinilunga District, is the last small north-western bulge of North-Western Province, in the clasp of Angola to the west and the Congo to north and east.

The Boma building was low, white-walled, wide-eaved. Khaki-uniformed police and Boma messengers in blue uniforms with red facings were clustered in the deep shade of the verandah. The D.S.

was gently welcoming—but no he had had no notice of our coming—and indeed, he had been installed there only two days. This was Lunda country, and he, who was from elsewhere, spoke not a word of Lunda. (In Zambia there are over ninety languages and dialects.) I explained that because it had been my intention to walk or go upon the river for all the journey, I needed bearers and a guide.

The D.S. was distressed, but, what could he do in these circumstances? However, he was earnest on our behalf, and it was so we came by George.

There was no warning in first sight of him. He was young, his large white smile in his black face was a little shy, and even, as I thought, innocent. The innocence was mine. His truck was a Toyota and had been a good strong truck. Now it was clapped out, and should have been a warning. On its doors was painted 'Welcome Tea Room'. Only in retrospect has the funniness of that emerged.

I thought George and his truck could serve the purpose that was to have been the bearers'. From the source to where the river leaves Zambia to enter Angola, is only about fifty miles—why shouldn't George pick us up from each day's walking to return us to a central base? At this stage I had to follow the river only to Angola's border. I would pick it up thereafter where it came out of Angola's southern frontier, back into Zambia.

The road out of Mwinilunga to the area of the source was not the best of dirt roads. All are very dusty and some uneven; this was humped, pitted, erratic, obtruded with rock. The truck's top speed was about fifty and George acknowledged no other. We bounded out of Mwinilunga, ricochetting metallically from rock to rock. Women and children saw us from afar and leaped like antelopes into the bush. In the cab we were shaken like stones in a can. I thought we could not arrive anywhere before the truck's abused old parts flew apart. But we did, and so it was that George

19

was waiting for us when we came out of the Congo and into Zambia by the Independence Monument.

We left the monument and, on the track, we had at first on the one side the Congo and on the other Zambia, thick forest both. Then we stopped.

'There's the frontier,' the guide said.

On the left a broad half grown-out clearing went beyond the reach of sight at right angles to the track. That was all. No sign, no soul but us. Beyond the clearing it was Zambia on both sides of the track. I got out to stare—I expect something of a frontier, the idea has drama. A frontier should have *some* expression of that, and most have. This one was doggedly uneventful and, seeking something to mark it with portent, I saw a small shrub with purple droplets of blossom.

'*Lupapi*,' the guide said, 'it is medicinal.'

Medicinal, so said, would mean that it has a part in the medicines of the witch doctors, and I clung to that. I must find something significant. Among frontiers, what could be more suggestive, more stimulating as an idea, than that of Zambia and the Congo, deep in the forested heart of Central Africa? But I could not complain. I had that day walked the infant river from its hidden source, and it, for much of the way, the frontier. There was drama enough.

After a few miles the track joined the main road, if such you could call the deeply dusty ten-foot way. It pushed from village to village through the bush with the high trees densely about it, clear-stemmed, heavy evergreen crowned, and under them smaller ones pendulous with blossom. The villages had pineapple plots and fleshy stands of bananas and, often, a large shrub with smooth, serpentine, jointed limbs. It was leafless, with hanging masses of brilliant flame-coloured flowers.

It was close to evening when we came to Ikelengi.

2

We stopped by the rest house in Ikelengi, under the great trees which shaded it and shaded the whole village. The village was so snuggled in green exuberance that although I could see it was large I could only guess its form and size. Then the brief twilight came and soon it was dark.

We were surrounded as soon as we stopped. The men were friendly and curious, and children laughed and pushed in inquisitive circles round us. They peered at my white face, nudging and chattering, but they were polite children. Some, whose English was good, spoke to us and then hid their faces in a confusion of giggles. Somebody fetched the man who had the key to the rest house, and I think he must have lived at a distant extremity of the village. They pushed and hustled him when he came.

This was a very simple rest house. It had four rooms ranged, bungalow-fashion, along a verandah facing on the central space of the village. When a paraffin pressure lamp was brought, Kay and I went gingerly to inspect the rooms; they were empty except for iron beds, two to a room. The dingy brown blankets were crumpled.

'Do you think there will be bed bugs?' Kay asked.

It looked possible. I said I would sleep on the bed, not in it—though that would really be no defence against the blood lust of bed bugs. But there was the floor—a floor, however hard, is better than bugs in a bed. But our suspicion was unworthy; there were no bugs. Rough the rest house was, but not dirty.

When we came out another man stood in the enclosure of light; the rest stood apart from him in a half circle of profound respect. He was large, broad, rather imposing, dressed very neatly in a white shirt and dark blue trousers. He was polite, smiling rather deprecatingly, but with easy authority.

'I am the chief. I am Chief Ikelengi. This is my village. You are strangers. I must know who you are and why you are here. That is important you see.'

We introduced ourselves while, still very politely, he scrutinized us. Then he smiled again and said we were welcome to Ikelengi. His manner was faintly courtly, and he was dignified, but amiable and easy. I told him of my journey and that we had that day come from the source of the Zambezi. He began to talk of the river, particularly of the source, and though our guide, one of his people, had been casual about it, he was mystical. I felt no less so.

'At the beginning, where the water starts, did you see the little fish?'

I said that yes, I had seen them, and had been surprised that they were there, in the first inches of the river.

'If you catch one of those fish you should not try to eat it. However much you cook it it will never die.'

I asked what was the reason for that and how did he know. He shook his head slowly, looking down, smiling with an inward air.

'I had that from my forefathers. They came from the Congo. We are the Ndembu people of the great Lunda tribe who came here from the Congo a long time ago, from the kingdom of Mwantiyanvwa. Mwantiyanvwa in the Congo is still our tribal centre—the heart of our people you know.'

The time of their coming, as he spoke of it, was like something immeasurably long since, but, as I learnt subsequently, it was about three hundred years ago—time that had done nothing to sever that ethnic link. It still pulls on their tribal consciousness. This part of Zambia, its final north-western extremity, is a meeting and mingling point. East and West Africa meet with a fusion of edges. Congo forest spills over the border as do some birds of West Africa. The Congo and the Zambezi have interchanged tributaries—there is, as geographers say, much evidence of river capture.

Chief Ikelengi had pride in his Lunda blood but told me earnestly and with no less pride of his part in the emergent nation of Zambia, so personifying his moment in African history. He was Lunda, emotionally rooted in the Congo, a chief in a district where change had impinged less and later than most parts of Zambia, but intellectually and at a different emotional level wholly committed to his part in the new nation.

In this Ndembu country old rituals and beliefs still contain the lives and imaginations of the people. Such avowal as *is* given to Christianity is the thinnest of skins over them. Chief Ikelengi had a modern look with his neat clothes and easy manner, but all the generations before were in him when he spoke of his people and the river. He was the living continuance of all that, but he told me with pride of his periodical visits to Lusaka to attend the Council of Chiefs. Through that he had his part in the making of the future, a total involvement in the progress of the nation. But neither he nor his people questioned the mystery of his authority.

They stood worshipfully in their distant half circle, heads bowed. He turned to them, unconsciously god-like, directing them for our care. Each man, as spoken to, sank to a reverential curtsy, with a soft double hand-clap, a touch on the thighs with flat hands, then another double hand-clap. Hand-clapping, in various forms and degrees, is common to many tribes for greeting from common respect to reverence. That for Chief Ikelengi was ultimate respect. I, no chief, was given the double hand-clap, a touching of the thighs and the repeated hand-clap, but no curtsy.

Chief Ikelengi, very erect, looked taller than his height among his genuflecting subjects. He received their obeisances absently, again casually god-like. Turning to us he said that, the next night, we must have dinner with him.

'And that,' I said to myself, 'is not an invitation. It is a gracious command.'

He left us. The sibilant night enclosed us. The men, speaking softly among themselves, were busy on our behalf, pulling together a little rough hearth of loose stones at the base of a great tree, blowing to life a fire of sticks. Then it was burning and bigger wood added and our cans, one of baked beans and one of stewed steak, tipped into a battered pan for heating. The men squatted round, aromatic smoke lay on the air; we sat in the dust drinking beer.

I have never been without respect for beer, but tropical Africa taught me unsuspected reaches of its virtue. In Africa beer is significant. It is woven through the rituals of social crisis— circumcision rites, initiation and curative rituals. It has to do with divinity and divination and the permanent mysteries. It runs through all mysticism and, walking and sweating and thirsting, I found it easy to become mystical about it. Often, at times of deprivation, Kay and I held wistful conversations about it.

We had beer now, a crate, which is a carton holding two dozen bottles. In the priorities of the bush there was no utter adversity while that lasted. You take the first one desperately, laving the gullet, taking it all almost in one grateful gulp. Then you sigh and settle to a more lingering pleasure. We sat in the soft dust very nearly without thought, smelling the aromatic fire, hearing sounds of the village beyond. We were hungry, furiously hungry—we had not eaten since the previous day. But food was necessity; beer was bliss.

When I first came to Africa I brought with me convictions about beer. I had certainty about its proper temperature—it should be about 54 degrees Fahrenheit for its best flavour and body to emerge. I came on that first trip with another man to make films, and if I could be said to be fond of beer, he was devout. Jointly and utterly we repudiated the African way. They drank it cold. Beer, we pontificated, should be warm and we insisted upon having it so. That caused wonder, even dismay, among those with whom we thirsted. They said we were odd and, as the climate's hot embrace had its way with me, I began to feel myself odd. Warm beer *was* flaccid on the palate, and I tried one cold. I never looked back. In Africa, like the rest, I speak not of 'a beer', but of 'a cold beer'. My friend stayed piously staunch and drank out the trip on warm beer. He was a martyr for his faith.

It had been another of my convictions that there were appropriate times for the drinking of beer, mainly middle day and evening. That too collapsed in Africa. There were no inappropriate times. Days start early in the bush; dawn comes, the hot day has begun, and you rise ready for the first one. There is a tantalizing pleasure in delaying it for the first hours.

Our food was taken from the fire, the mess of it tipped on two old enamel plates. Without bread or any other insulation it was ready for us. I looked at it, smelt it, and my ravening hunger fell faint and died. If you are hungry enough, it is said, you will eat anything. I was not hungry enough. There was not much of that food with its spurious swill of gravy, but it was that much ahead of desire. Say it is fuel I said to myself, and began to force it down, trying to swallow without tasting it.

We did our best, then sat on the edge of the verandah with the beer. The children had gone and the men too; the village was silent. It was about half past eight and nobody wakeful but us.

There was no more human sound, but the darkness was enormously secret with sound. Cicadas shrilled as they do day and night, with high fever and the air rustled with the millions-strong flight of insects drawn by the light. Some looked fearsomely venomous, and perhaps they were, though many a harmless creature has a protective look of ferocity. You cannot be sure unless

25

you can identify the individual and when a huge hornet-like thing settled on my knee I did not provoke it. A patina of insects wrapped every surface, among them as always the praying mantises waiting in frozen postures.

The frogs were in full chorus; their high rather watery singing was, as it may often be, quite musical, throbbing and wavering, and somewhere that night a bass group was rumbling with the rest.

In the immensity of the night the sounds went on and on, throbbing and shrilling, and in all that thronging I had the sense that we were invisible onlookers.

The glow died from the fire and we went to our rooms. We had sat there for an eternity, but it was only about ten o'clock. I scrutinized the bed, sniffed for scent of bugs, lay on the bed and, sweating peacefully, went to sleep.

When I woke the air and light were thin with morning. Pale light flared up the sky but the sun had not yet risen above the trees. A few rangy dogs scoured for muck and the first women were carrying water, carrying it on their heads in calabashes, walking with a superb erect sway. It was soon after five.

I walked slowly, and, stirring the dust and parting the scratching hens, I thought of how explosive a push this modest track had brought to history here. There had been no road till, in recent times, this one had been pushed out from Mwinilunga through the Ndembu country. It had brought more change than ever had been seen before. But I could not think too profoundly about that or anything else. There was too much elation in the morning.

The air was clean and soft and, so early, cool, not yet eighty degrees. Everything was pointed with a rapturous lucidity. Under the trees the huts and houses squatting for shade were neat and thatched and good, trim in the shining morning.

The rolling piccaninns had begun to emerge into the light and, as the sun came above the trees, I came back to the rest house. Kay was there and a man was urging life into the fire against the tree. He brought us warm water, in our turns, two inches in an old aluminium bowl. He would have heated breakfast for us too, the stuff of the night before, but though hunger gnawed, so did queasy distaste.

Now nearly six, it was full day. The men had gathered again and the children, bolder now, had brought their exercise books for us to see. They showed them shyly, and seeing them so good and neat I asked inwardly why that should astonish me. But this *was* the heart of Central Africa. Old mysteries, old beliefs and practices *are* still dominant. However, change is licking into the remotest places, and the front of it is education. Every day everywhere in Zambia children walk the roads and tracks to bush towns where the schools are. One boy, about ten and tall and slight, spoke beautiful English. His writing was even and clean and his spelling impeccable. He is part of the paradox too, I told myself, like Chief Ikelengi. Magical beliefs and fears still dominate the world of his brief life, but he has his other foot firmly in the future.

The children talked to us in English. The men beyond, among themselves, spoke Lunda.

'Do you know,' Kay said, 'I don't understand one word they say, not one word. I speak my own language, Lozi, and several other Zambian languages, and everywhere in Zambia I've been able to understand and be understood whether I speak the local language or not—but here—not one word.'

The ethnic frontier again. Speech belonged to the Congo and— a bewitching debt—so did the costume of the women. They were superb, those women, erect and lissom in their brilliant clothes.

Their headdresses were elaborate, finely contrived as crowns. Their purpose was simply to soften the weight of full calabashes, but so artfully done as to seem to have no purpose but to be beautiful. A main garment, boldly striped or medallioned, reached the ankles, and over that another as brilliant was caught round the waist, tucked there and hanging to the calves.

Such traditional costume is not universal in Zambia. Many women in other areas do wear what is approximately that, but without its exultant beauty, or the superb wearing of it. Beautiful women are not uncommon in other tribes, and sometimes they are beautifully dressed; but the Ndembu women are transcendent.

In Ikelengi there was a foil for their beauty. They glided by, singly or in twos and threes; beyond them across the open area there was a store, brick-built, concrete-faced, roofed with asbestos. It was solid, stolid, practical, ugly and symbolic. So were the Coca-Cola advertisements on the walls. They could stand for much of the effect of Western colonization. The missionaries had come and with them commercial exploitation, and the result had been not wholly bad and far from wholly good. Whatever the benefits the effect upon indigenous culture had been hideously degenerative.

3

George and his truck took us out of Ikelengi. We bounded out, scattering the hens and flaying the morning's peace with screams of clapped-out metal. As we hurtled down the road taking bumps and holes in gangling leaps women and children scurried into the bush far ahead. They were wise, wiser than I knew. George was to take us to the river downstream of our first day's progress and from there we would walk, to be picked up later for return to Ikelengi. But George had neglected to carry reserves of petrol. He said we must seek that first—and my faint faith in the vehicle could too easily imagine an empty tank.

The great farm owned by an English family would have petrol, George was sure. Certainly they would let us have some. When we reached it it looked snug and splendid enough for any need, fenced and tended and impeccable, very Britishly settled and sound. The house showed above a towering hedges swagged with bougainvillea and ipomoea and through the drive-in I could see ranks of frangipani and hibiscus. Under the eucalyptus trees the house was as English as an apple orchard. We waited and I, now sickly hungry, felt a waif.

We may have looked like waifs. When the owner came, tall, very English, he regarded us distantly.

'Petrol? No. Rains have started. Roads soon be bad—shan't be able to get through. Only enough for ourselves.'

He turned and walked away.

George, not a man to be needlessly humbled, took us humbly

now till, free of the aura, he revived. There was the school, he said, Sakeji School.

That was different; I felt its sense of welcome at once though there was not a soul to be seen. It had a secret air. We came to it by a turning track of soft dust under high shrubs and parked the truck against a banana thicket. It was silent, and we stood in the sun. The heavy sweetness of frangipani lay on the air.

A great empty open space was ranged at the sides with low buildings with arched and colonnaded façades, and there was not sight or sound of a human being. We waited and I had the sense that we were seen and received though not yet met.

Then on the far side a figure tiny with distance came out of the colonnaded shadow and advanced, silhouetted in the brilliance. We met in the hot empty centre.

He was very courteous, old-fashionedly formal at first, with a soft American accent. Why yes, certainly we could have petrol and he led us to a storage tank. He talked urbanely while our tanks were filled—he was Mr Hess, for thirty years principal of the school and its founder, and it was he who had designed the buildings and the whole complex.

It was a school for children of missionaries. He took us into the classrooms, and the children, a few African, the rest white, smiled and greeted us politely.

I smelt the bakery before we came to it, a good smell anywhere at any time, but now I yearned in response. We were very hungry. A recurrent vertigo confused me and Kay was visibly struggling for a show of normality. I heard myself say, as from a distance, how good the bread looked. I tried not to snatch the loaf that Mr Hess offered.

'It is our custom,' he said, 'for all the staff to meet at this time in the morning for coffee. Perhaps you would care to join us?'

Coffee! Steaming and milky! Biscuits too perhaps.

'Thank you, that would be very pleasant,' I said, striving to be casually polite.

Kay, who had been silent till then, spoke. 'Oh yes thank you, that would be nice.'

Mr Hess's living-room was spacious, the armchair ineffably comfortable, and there was the coffee tray coming in. I think it was good coffee but I was not critical. It soothed and irradiated, quelled the gnawing. There *were* biscuits.

The nagging eased, conversation became possible. In the upholstered tranquillity the fair girl was telling me that her home was in the county of Dorset and Dorset shares a border with my own county of Wiltshire. It was unreal, with the hot bush filling the horizons outside.

We stepped more strongly, Kay and I, outside again, able to follow the ambling pleasure of Mr Hess's conversation.

'Our own little river,' he said as we came to a stream shallow among the stones,' the Sakeji River—the very first tributary of any consequence of the Zambezi.

'And d'you see that tree, it's *muShukota*, a lovely timber tree, used for furniture you know. Ah, and do you see that one with its very elaborately furrowed bark—that's *muLombwa*, most widely useful.'

I knew the tree. *MuLombwa* is its Bemba name. I had known it in Barotse country and its name there, a Lozi one, is *muKwa*. The bark is very deeply furrowed, rather scaly; it exudes a gummy fluid, brilliantly blood-red, which is the reason for its being woven through many of the rituals. It symbolizes blood, particularly menstrual blood. The bark, and the root, are used in the medicines of witch doctors, and the sap, toxic, with a stupefying action, is used in the catching of fish. The timber is good—the sapwood pinkish and olivaceous, flecked with crimson, the heartwood hard and brown and beautifully responsive to the carver's gouge. From a log of it I carved a portrait head of Kay.

We left Mr Hess reluctantly. We passed back, so to speak, through the looking glass. George dropped us as near the river as his truck would go—there was a bridge downstream, he said, by Nkomba village. He would wait for us there.

We found such way as we could by the river, walking its rapidly widening reaches. It was gaining size and strength, going in throaty rushes, hanging in pools. In all the miles we saw not one human being nor any game.

We had eaten some of the bread, but hunger can be overborne by thirst. The bread clogged in our kiln-dry mouths. We talked of guinea fowl, making a fantasy of that to torment ourselves. We saw none.

In the highest heat of afternoon we came to the bridge by Nkomba village. There was a minor throng there. Below the bridge the river widened abruptly at its sides, making crystalline pools in rock basins especially, as it seemed, for the frolicking of the people. They paddled and plunged in uproarious bliss, the women and the naked piccaninns, shrieking and chattering and falling into huge laughter. Among all those fine black laughing faces I think I, for all my sunburn looked funnily fair, and that added to the laughter. But they were friendly, ready to laugh at or with anybody—it was wonderful to be playing in the cool clear water, not remembering the moment gone or anticipating one to come. George was there, but did not seem to be quite in the spirit of it. He stood about.

And there was the bridge, the first over the great Zambezi River. Its three piers were caged with neatly interlayered logs, the cages packed with rocks. Great logs, whole boles, spanned from pier to pier and over that a transverse layer of massive baulks that made the surface.

It was pleasant there, a place to dally, pleasanter than the road's receding blaze of distance; but we had to be back in Ikelengi by evening. We must be prompt for dinner with the chief. I thought allowance should be made for the truck's uncertainty and that doubt was justified within minutes. It checked, coughed several times, then stopped. While George beat under the bonnet with a heavy spanner, we sat in the cab easing the hot wet cling of our clothes. Unreasonably the truck returned to life, but it was tenuous. We punctuated the miles with stops.

Hunger was forgotten now, thirst possessed us utterly, all else was submerged by the vast craving. There was a store in a village someone told us, and we diverged miles to find it. It was shut, a little shanty shut and shuttered, and anyway, they told us round-about, there was no beer in the village. But, randomly as we now searched for beer, I cannot guess how we came to be on the road to Mwinimilambo. The map does not suggest any logical course that could have taken us there.

But on it we were, headed away from any way we should be going. Then the truck coughed again and, apparently finally, died. George tinkered, beat with the spanner, but there was no answering stir of life. We stood by, thinking of beer.

Then I thought I must be thirstier than I had thought, hallucinated. Coming towards us on this remote rough track in the scorching wilderness was a white woman on a bicycle, erect, with serene leisurely pedalling. She was neatly and cleanly dressed in a rather old-fashioned summer dress. She stopped and smiled, stepping down from her high bicycle and speaking with an Australian accent.

'Broken down? There's a village a few miles up the road—you could probably get help.' Then, looking at us, 'And something to drink.'

She smiled again, remounted the very upright machine and pedalled placidly away.

'Thank you,' I said vaguely to her trim departing back. 'We'll go there.'

She must be real I thought. Kay had seen her too. We began to walk. We left George with his dead truck.

I cannot estimate the miles of that road. They were probably not many, but the sun's glare pressed on us, our tongues swelled. We walked with no sense of reducing distance. Sometimes the road rose, sometimes declined, sometimes it was flat; but always, interminably, it stretched ahead. I could not believe we would ever do anything else but walk under that incandescence. When at last we came upon the women an end became a possibility.

The three of them carried great bundles of cassava sticks, in single file, swaying easily up the road under their immense burdens. They talked incessantly in a high shrill trialogue. They did not appear to see us, greatly heightening my sense of hallucination. So we are ghosts, I thought, dead of thirst. From time to time they stopped to rest, not putting down their burdens but extending them and their arms vertically above their heads to ease their necks.

Their presence suggested that the village could not be too far off, and there were cassava plots. We were ascending a long slight rise. Beyond that perhaps, the village? Not too soon. My legs were rubbery, my sight fuzzed. Kay's head was drooping, her knees bending weakly. We staggered slightly as we entered the village.

And there was a store. We headed for it. It was shut. Beyond, at the village's further end, there was a group, men and women gossiping. We tried without much success to reach understanding —one intimated that he spoke Nyanja (or it may have been Kaonde), but Kay, who did, could understand no word of his. Then, in deadlock, he signed to us to follow him. He did convey to us that he was taking us to the chief.

Chief Mwinimilambo was in his enclosure with his wives. He rose with great courtesy, greeting us with the rather courtly dignity shown by Chief Ikelengi. In good English he asked us what brought us there; could it be his pleasure to help us? We explained that, primarily, we were thirsty; secondarily that George and the dead truck were down the road.

He bowed. 'Come to my house.'

It was in the centre of the village, spaced a little apart from the rest. We went up the steps and over the verandah and into a quite large room sparsely furnished in European style. In a smaller room beyond he showed us a row of calabashes against the wall.

'See,' he said, 'honey beer. We brew it today to drink tomorrow. It is good. It will take away your thirst.'

Carrying a calabash he ushered us to a sofa in the living-room and there filled a large glass jug from the calabash. Slowly, with some ceremony, he poured a glass and drank it. He paused, looked at us and smiled. As traditional courtesy required he had shown the beer was good, not poisoned. Now he topped up the jug, from that refilled the tumbler, gave it to Kay. It was cloudy, greyish-yellow, with floating particles. Kay drank and a suffusion of bliss came upon her.

She drained the glass and it was my turn. Never had drink been better. It was cool, undoubtedly beer, but with a tang that then was exquisite—even on subsequent and less poignantly thirsty occasions it was hardly less so. Then it was Kay's turn again, and so, turn and turnabout till the jug was empty, all the time under the avuncular watching of Chief Mwinimilambo. It was a large jug and the beer was potent. We had staggered slightly coming in; though refreshed we staggered slightly going out. If Chief Mwinimilambo noted that I think he thought it proper.

He had said that he could send someone to help with the truck, but, when we came out, there was George and the truck. Ailing though the truck was, it lived on.

Brief twilight was sinking into night when we reached Ikelengi, so late that I feared Chief Ikelengi would think us discourteous.

We sent a messenger and awaited our summons. and in half an hour it came. Led by a man with a lamp we were conducted to the chief's house. He received us on the verándah, chiding gently. 'You did not come. I had my dinner.' But he was gracious when we explained. 'I will have dinner again, with you,' he said kindly, and led us to his sitting-room. A portrait of the president looked down upon the Edwardian furnishings. We sat on a sofa while he instructed the obeisant half-circle of servants. Each, when spoken to, gave the double hand-clap, the touch on the thighs, the repeated hand-clap, with meek uplifted eyes. Still half-bent they shuffled to the kitchen. We waited for dinner and the chief talked with slow urbanity, of his people, of the past, and I wish obsessional hunger had not prevented my following and remembering the whole of it. He showed us, on the wall, the yellowing photograph of his father in the full state of the old days, telling us of those times; but my stomach was metronomically counting off the moments till we should be called to the table. When the curtsying servant came to summon us we rose promptly, Kay and I.

Chief Ikelengi led us past the genuflecting staff in the kitchen, to the dining-room. We had had a precautionary beer at the rest house and, no longer thirsty, responded excruciatingly to the entry of the food, boiled chicken, piled high, a huge dish of potatoes, all excellently cooked. How well the chief had dined before we came I do not know, but he paced us well, talking with affable ease. I hope it was not too uncomfortable a courtesy for him. I think he was politely anxious that our wolfish appetites should not embarrass us.

I hope too that we sensed aright the time for departure. We had returned to the sitting-room and not long after rose to go. It was about eight o'clock. The day was over; as we walked back through the thrumming darkness few lamps were still burning. Sleep was settling on Ikelengi.

36

The sun's early blaze was climbing the sky when we left the village next morning. George's truck, extraordinarily quick with gangling life again, ejected us not far from the river and left us in the grateful hush. So early the day's heat had not accumulated. We had had no breakfast and could not guess when we would eat again, but now we had energy from the last evening's dinner. We were content. The world was lovely in the young morning and we stepped lightly.

Hereabouts, they had said, there were guinea fowl and, light-heartedly, we thought that a promise. In the outcome in all that day not a feather of one did we see—but, in bushwacking, you count only current moments.

The river was enlarging prodigiously, the banks reaching apart till, at mid-morning, a full hundred yards, and often more, of tumbling flow ran between them. Above the first bridge it had been, mostly, quite gentle, but now in its gathering strength we came to the first major rapids. The turmoil poured down a bouldery confusion for a mile, with pauses in agate pools which shattered in tossing runs. Caught in the elation of it, we watched for a long time.

Then Kay sighed and, looking down, stepped back quickly.

'Look!' she said. In a pool at her feet was a snake, nine inches long, bright green and slender. It was dead. I guessed uncertainly —a very small green mamba? A boomslang? Or perhaps a western green snake, which is harmless; the other two are deadly.

But whichever it was, there it was at least visible. Others were possibly wreathed in almost every tree we passed under and coiled under as many stones. But whatever is believed in less infested places, snakes are seldom aggressive. The snake that strikes is one that is, or feels itself to be, molested. Snakes will avoid man if they may, as will most wild animals. That is as accurately a part of the ecological balance as other factors—if mambas were aggressive they would make serious inroads on human population. Death comes soon from their bite because the venom, a nerve poison, prevents the functioning of the lungs. It induces suffocation.

At a fishing camp by Lake Tanganyika in Zambia's northernmost extremity there was a jetty roughly built of boulders, and many of the cells of its honeycomb structure gave harbourage to water cobras. There must have been hundreds, and some were huge. Every day, going to the boats, we walked the jetty, but were never attacked.

A small electric motor on the jetty which pumped water to the camp stood on two stones under a canvas cover, and one of the men, taking off the cover one morning, leapt backwards. His yell of fright brought us running. Under the motor, between the stones, a huge cobra was coiled. It was asleep.

We looked at it, not competing for action. The camp manager reached with a pole to dislodge the motor so that it should fall on the snake. At the instant of touch it exploded into lightning life— so did we. But we need not have jumped. In a moment's movement it had slid over the edge, into a hole.

We made good progress through this rather easier country, lightly wooded, grassy between the trees. Recurrent vistas filled with sky and the shine of water overwhelmed with a sense of space. We went ant-like, none but us in so much space.

We found humanity again in the afternoon. George, with the truck at our rendezvous. Back on the dusty red road we came to a village. At its entrance, by the road, a small wooden platform stood on a post. On the platform stood an empty bottle. That signified that beer was in the village. We stopped.

The village disgorged its people, the men, the jostling chatter of children, and, hovering uncertainly behind, the women. I gave the double hand-clap and the whole throng returned it, the children coming close and lifting beaming faces. We pointed to the bottle —had they beer? They brought it, honey beer, and watched us drink.

38

Bonhomie was now established and uproarious. A man whose English was modestly practical said he was going to teach me Lunda. He began at once. But perhaps, I said, the present opportunity would not take me far. Perhaps I should get a book. He held up his hand. 'Wait,' he said, and ran.

In moments he was back, waving a book, paper-covered, thumbed and worn. It was a Lunda-English Dictionary.

'It is my own book—see, here on the cover I have written my name.'

N. Kasekeli the signature read.

'Does it give all the important words?'

He flipped the pages, then stabbed with his finger. *Kasolu* the word read, honey beer. He showed it to everyone else too, and there was unanimity that this was a most useful beginning for me. We all had some more honey beer to signify that. He allowed me to buy the book for two Kwacha, and we were both well satisfied with the bargain.

Among the children a little girl, two at a guess, was carried by her elder sister. She was eating a green mango, and green mangoes are well known not to be good for tummies of tiny girls. She burst into tears when I tried to make friends with her.

'She is not really unfriendly,' her sister told me, 'she thinks you want her green mango.'

Drawn by the loud weeping, mother came, and was persuaded that green mangoes are not good for little girls. She took it. When, soon after, we left the village, the last sound of it was the bitter wailing of the deprived little girl.

Villages were frequent on the road, some a cluster of half a dozen huts, some larger, but collectively enough to make a fairly constant coming and going. As we hurtled ahead of our red dust cloud, panic went before us. Adults and children far ahead leaped for the security of the bush. Why, I asked Kay, should they be *so* afraid?

Perhaps George had driven that road before, leaving a memory reason enough for fear. People were not the only stragglers—the chicken showed as wholesome a panic as the people, and they left it later to flap squawking away, and, finally, too late. A cock and two hens scratched intently by the verge; they paid no heed. George swung the wheel. We lurched into the verge. Behind us three bloody feathery bundles were left strewn on the road.

George smiled a little and said nothing when we turned furiously upon him.

But for a while he made no more attempts on chicken; probably he felt us relax. We were taken unawares when we came up upon a woman walking ahead at the roadside. She, unlike the rest, did not leap for safety. At the last moment George swung the wheel. In the violent swing and sideways bouncing of the truck I could not tell if he had caught her. I peered back—she was standing, rigid with terror.

Our horror and anger may have impinged upon George—or our threat of invoking authority. For the rest of the way to Ikelengi he drove circumspectly.

4

Kalene Hill Mission is remote; as remote, I suppose, as a mission in Zambia could be. It lies in the last outer tip of North-Western Province, just a few miles from Angola to the west, and as few from the Congo to the north, just perched there. But the Zambezi traveller following the river from the source to its exit to Angola comes there inevitably.

When you come it encloses you; it is so clean and clinical and quietly ordered that it excludes the sense of the hot wild bush outside. Its roads and paths run spaciously and its buildings are set about widely. But it is an enclosure; in the eye of that African sun its coolness and calm are alien.

It had many of the aspects of missionary activity which can keep an observer, free from bias as he may be, in a state of oscillation. This mission, as the whole principle of missions must be, *was* alien. For good or ill missions are an unassimilable grafting upon the living body of Africanism. All missions perform a medical function and beyond question have so brought incalculable benefit. The greater part of Kalene Hill is a hospital, a big and impeccable one by African standards so far. To belittle the work of such places would be misrepresentative.

But that is only a part of the truth—missionaries are by definition workers in a religious crusade. However great the good they have done by medical ministry, religious inculcation is part of the same package. The missionaries of the nineteenth century found 'Darkest Africa' and sought to change it. They found it primitive, pagan, woven through with sorcery and witch doctoring. From that they assumed an innate moral inferiority in the black man which it must be their mission to uplift. From their total assumption that theirs was the only possible and whole truth, it seemed that they had found a people in a state of darkest heathen forsakenness.

Some of the Christian innovators were well-intentioned but because they would have thought it irrelevant they took no perceptive account of traditional values and practices. They had no conception that African beliefs were a growth of the African situation and met African needs. The missionaries' Christian ethic, imposed intact, was alien and at least in part irrelevant. However magically decked out the practices of witch doctors were, and are, for many circumstances they are an effective means of discovering hidden stresses that produce personal and social maladjustments. There *is* much mystical belief in illness caused by persecution by dead kin, and no doubt the early missionaries judged it black superstition. But it is no harder to accept than some of the beliefs of orthodox Christianity. Understanding was the more difficult because those early reformers believed without question that the moral virtues were exclusive to Christianity.

In truth, in that original Africa the factors of environment were master to all and remained so whatever the cult acknowledged. The African cults were more realistic. Man, like a leech or a lion, had to survive in a predatory ecology. His beliefs, his rituals, his moral code were born of that. How oddly insubstantial the first preachings must have seemed among the hot realities!

So far the oil and water of Christian and African morality were not particularly damaging. In sexual morality they were. Man, said the missionaries, has two natures—the spiritual one, noble and 'pure', and the physical one, intrinsically deplorable. The duty of the first is to keep the second down in the pit in which it belongs. The spiritual self must make life-long expiation for the possession of sexual instincts. The nineteenth-century pioneers were free of doubt. Sex was sin. In black Africa there was work to do. Here were people with no segregation of sex. It was good to see the sun at morning, to smell the earth when the rains came, to eat, to have babies and find joy in the other sex. The body, as the means of so much that was good, was carried proudly and nakedly. That, said the early missionaries, was barbarous depravity.

The effect of that teaching has been curiously uneven. Pride of body has been a casualty, polygamy, largely, has not. Though the rituals still have their symbolism of fertility and unaffected sex, there may be an almost exaggerated selfconsciousness about the body. The ritual glorifies the body, the shame degrades it.

At Kalene Hill Mission we were conducted on a tour by an English woman, whom I will call Miss Wentworth. Miss Wentworth was laconic, matter-of-fact, and splendid. Whatever may be the general effect of missionaries, I think it impossible that she could have brought anything but good.

When we had toured the general wards we came to a steel-framed, steel-meshed door fastened with a padlock. Miss Wentworth unlocked it.

'Have to do this you know—don't want trouble. The maternity ward you see. The young men.'

From there she led us to buildings rather apart from the rest.

'Leprosy department. Come and meet our lepers.'

They stood and sat and squatted at the doors, some without hands or feet, some with grossly disfigured faces, but cheerful, apparently happy.

'Can't do anything about those injuries—the disease is stopped though. It's not the leprosy that does that damage, it's having no feeling there—they burn themselves and hurt themselves on things. I think they're pretty happy here.'

They were affectionate towards her, smilingly polite to us.

'Now I'll show you our witches' village.'

She led us away from the hospital buildings to a secluded place screened by mat fencing. Within it lay the village, a miniature of those of that area, the buildings of big sun-baked bricks, the food store on legs, everything as it would be outside. The women squatted, pealing cassava root. They were old, saggingly wizened, unquestionably witch-like.

'They're all witches—or anyway, said to be. It's hard to tell. They were cast out of the villages and lucky to get here really. Would have been killed if they'd been caught—ritual killing you know, strangled. They'll spend the rest of their lives here. Look about ninety don't they? Not as old as they look though—probably only about sixty.'

'How were they identified as witches?'

'Oh—I expect the witch doctor pointed them out—or they may have failed a test. They get chickens and appoint one to any woman accused of witchcraft. Then they give the chickens poison and if one dies its owner is proved guilty. There was one found guilty that way and fled from the village to come here. Never reached here though—caught and strangled.

'You see that one over there? When she came here I asked her why she'd been accused. "I ate a person," she said—that means she'd eaten the spirit of the person, and that means he'd die.

'And that one there, you see? Said to have eaten the spirit of her pregnant daughter. Anyway the girl died. Told me she was innocent when she came here—"Why should I do that to my own daughter?" she said to me. But on the day the girl died and this woman was accused, the girl's husband took their other child to his own village—but almost at once he and the child died too. You just can't tell.'

Through Miss Wentworth I asked one of the women her age. She shook her head; she had no idea how long she had lived.

Witchcraft and sorcery, Miss Wentworth said, were so darkly

prevalent in that district that she could not be positive about the innocence or guilt of any such women. The terror of it veined the whole of life in the villages. One of the commonest beliefs is that people become possessed by the malevolently motivated spirits of ancestors. To placate them, and evil spirits of other kinds, huts are dedicated to them, set about outside with all sorts of totems.

The case of the woman said to have eaten her pregnant daughter illustrates the supposed nature and practices of witches and sorcerers. They have familiars, beings with the function of implementing their owners' evil purposes, and visible only to their owners or to a doctor who exorcises them. The visible form is variable, sometimes of animals, of dwarfed men with backward-pointing feet, of other queerly fearsome things. But their most terrifying quality is of being able to act of their own volition, often contrary to their owners' wishes—the more so because they are actuated by extremes of jealous malice. It leads them particularly to the killing of maternal kin and their husbands, and their owners' husbands—as in the case of the pregnant daughter. Subsequently, so the belief is, witch and familiar unearth the buried bodies of their victims, then devour them.

Sorcerers produce their own familiars, making them from evil medicines. For witches there is no such choice. Liking it or not they inherit their familiars from dead witch relatives—they are selected by the familiars. These beliefs, out of their context, appear to be only for the very credulous; in it, they have a terrifying reality. Real or imaginary as the gnawing horror may be, people die of it.

The term 'witch doctor' as usually used is loose and misleading; it includes all kinds from 'doctor' to sorcerer.

'We must get the witch doctor,' people say in any sort of adversity, and he, coming with his medicines, is one who cures —healing illness, exorcising bad spirits, being a conductor for the salient events of life. His means is ritual. In practice 'he' may be more than one person.

If, as the Ndembu say, a person is 'afflicted'—by illness, by possession by a spirit, by the malign work of a witch or sorcerer, the relatives will consult a diviner. His is the task of divining the cause and nature of the affliction; he does so by a ritualistic use of medicines. Divination done, a doctor wise in that particular form of affliction—a specialist—is consulted.

He brings a team of 'adepts' and to each gives a part according to his experience, gained as a patient or novice. The medicines, leaves, roots, bark, fruit, are subtly charged with symbolism, which in turn may be modified by the mode of use. A typical curative ritual is *Ihamba*.

The patient is one afflicted by the spirit of a dead hunter and in his body is hidden a tooth of the hunter. The name of the tooth is *Ihamba*, and thus of the ritual.

It is long, very complicated with its mystical and highly symbolic uses of medicines and, as it would seem, with a good deal of suffering for the patient. There is much ceremonial mixing of his blood with medicines.

Incisions are made at a number of places on his back and neck—usually done nowadays with a razor blade—and cupping horns applied. They are tips of goat horns, the ends cut off and plugged with beeswax, sucked on so that they grip. They fill with blood, sometimes fragments of flesh, then from time to time fall off. When they do the contents are put into calabashes to mix with the medicines there. Where they do, at the incisions, great weals are left. But perhaps the patient has little direct pain after the early stages because for much of the time he is in a state of partial trance, with violent ecstasies of trembling which pass at last into complete disassociation.

Then as he writhes and twitches the doctor takes from him a cupping horn and puts it and its spilling blood into a skin purse.

46

With rushing excitement he throws that into a calabash of mixed blood and medicine.

This is the climax. In the course of the ritual till now concealed resentments and stresses between the patient and his community have been drawn to light and, by exposure, dissipated. Now the doctor gropes in the bloody amalgam in the calabash until, triumphantly, he withdraws his hand holding a human tooth. He has 'caught' the *Ihamba*.

Now all is relaxed peace. The patient, so recently transported, sits tranquilly with the others, with much show of easy warmth between him and those for whom he had had crippling resentment.

Ihamba is a means of restoring to normality that which has been abnormal. The rituals of life crises are a signifying of the phases of what is normal. The chief ones are *Mukanda*, the circumcision ritual of boys, and *Nkang'a*, the puberty ritual of girls. Both symbolize the end of one phase of life and the beginning of another —the end of childhood, the dawn of adulthood. *Nkang'a* is the more pregnant for Lunda society as it is matrilineal—succession, inheritance, genealogy is through the maternal side. And for a very good reason say the Ndembu. There is no denying maternal blood, but who can swear with certainty to a person's paternity?

There are similar parallels to *Nkang'a* in many of Zambia's tribes—and probably elsewhere in Africa too. *Nkang'a* has one difference, so far as I know, from others—*when* it is performed. Most tribes so mark the girl's first menstruation. Among the Ndembu just *before* is the time and the criterion is the development of the breasts. Most tribes too regard the puberty ritual as complete in itself, with no necessary link with marriage, and with Ndembu this is now often so. But not traditionally. It has been the way that the whole course of *Nkang'a* had its termination in marriage.

The first part is *Kwing'ija*, and the first part of that is to take beer to the chief. That gains his permission for the ritual. Then the bridegroom gives arrows to the girl's mother and to the instructress who is to prepare her for the ritual and marriage. That is his symbol of masculinity; the bow, with its curves, signifies femininity. He also gives the instructress a calabash of beer. Now the shades—ancestor spirits—must be invoked and the village headman must do that after sunset in the presence of the girl and her mother. It is done before the village tree shrine. The girl kneels, open hands on the ground. There is much care, as there is at subsequent stages, to seek by invocation protection against sorcerers and witches who might take so vulnerable a time for the wreaking of evil. Now the girl is led by her mother into the bush where there is a *mudyi* sapling. Round that the ritual of the following day will centre, and it will have been previously selected by the instructress, the only other person who goes with the girl now. The *mudyi* has profound significance, and to go so, with no others, gives certainty that there shall be no witches or sorcerers present. They circle the *mudyi* three times, and *that* guards against the familiars of evilly intentioned persons.

It also renders the place sacred, as it must be for the initiation of the novice to be safe from all ill chance. Now she must fast, and so she will all through the next day's events. They start early, before sunrise.

The instructress and a few maternal women relatives go to the *mudyi* sapling. The novice goes too, but alone. She wears only a small cloth for her loins and her head is covered by a blanket. Now, and until the end, her whole conduct is circumscribed by taboos; one is that she shall not see the *mudyi*. The instructress lights a fire of peeled white sticks. The girl, under her hooding blanket, holds it to her with clenched hands against her temples, and looks only at the fire. She sits on an antelope hide (it must not be spotted or striped); the women go singing twice round

Emerging from the forest

Rapids near the source

the *mudyi*. She sings with them, heartily. It is the last sound she may utter. It is a taboo that after the fire has been lit she is compelled to silence.

Now, as the sun rises, the people of the village are fetched. The instructress spreads the antelope skin closely against the *mudyi* and on that she spreads the girl's blanket. Some of the women carry the girl from the fire to lay her on the blanket. The way of doing it has high significance. She is put on her left side with legs doubled back in the position of an unborn child. This is the 'dying place' (alternatively 'suffering place', apt for what is to follow).

It is the 'dying place' because, ritualistically, this marks the end of her first life. Childhood is over. She must die to be reborn into her second life, adulthood. With her clenched hands still at her temples she is covered by the blanket, completely tucked up. There now she must lie. There is a stringent taboo against her making any movement for the day's length till sundown. Hungry, stiff, painful, as she may become—*must* become—so she must stay, silent. As the women sing the instructress tells the novice of the punishments that will fall upon her if she breaks the taboo.

It is the time for singing and dancing now, and for much sharply pointed fun (for all but the novice) and till noon only the women dance. They start slowly, circling the novice. Two women lead the singing, loudly and stridently. The morning grows, more women come, many with slung babies, the pace increases, and the songs acidify. The men stand off, drink beer, deride the women who, now, are joyously scandalous. They sing of marriage, lampooning it; they praise the pleasures of adultery. They are, as it would be said in the West, beautifully bawdy.

'The girl is making a mistake at the beads,' they sing, and that refers to the string of beads worn round the waist, under the clothes. Then they sing 'O the stick of the *Chikinta* drum', and that refers to the male sexual organ. They sing with unction of the delights of illicit love, a sharper pleasure than conjugal love. They enjoy themselves enormously.

There is a change at noon, and a small relief for the poor novice under the blanket. She is turned with ceremony to her other side. The morning on her left side has represented femininity; to lie now on her right side represents masculinity. Her shoulder is rubbed to ease her stiffness.

The first man joins the dancing. He comes carrying a meal basket and after him a woman carrying one loaded with lumps of termite hill.

'The weight of the basket is killing me,' sing the women, and the allusion is that the basket is made heavier as a man is heavy.

Women take leaves from the bushes, scattering them, to give women the luck of being highly procreative; for the same purpose a basket of leaves is passed round the dancing circle of women. They show great pleasure, demonstrating the prevailing hunger for fertility.

All dance now, men and women, and the nature of the songs has changed, no longer scandalous, praising fertility. A woman plays a drum—it is open at one end and has within it a reed which, as she rubs it with a wet cloth, produces a grunting sound. It represents people in the throes of love. So it continues till about four o'clock.

Then it is time for the erection of the seclusion hut, nearly time for freeing the girl from her ordeal. Her suffering has been a symbol, a public one, to demonstrate that life's pleasures are counterbalanced by its sufferings, that you must suffer to earn pleasure. The bawdy songs and dances of the morning had their purpose—an airing of the fumes of illicit desires to ease the pressure of them for the better maintenance of social order and continuance.

The seclusion hut is set up at the further end of the village, almost into the bush. Its basis is, of course, symbolic—two poles of *mudyi* thrust into the ground on opposite sides of the circular plan. Their tops are drawn together and bound so that, by their angle of joining, they represent the human leg fork. More poles are added and the whole thatched with grass. Now, and until sunset, the women have a symbolic ceremony of eating.

Sunset brings relief·at last for the novice. On the back of the instructress and covered by her blanket, she is borne from her place of ordeal surrounded by the women. She must not be seen by the men who wait in the village centre where the drums are. The women dance and sing as they go, even the instructress carrying the girl, and each of them clutches in her hand a *mudyi* leaf to symbolize an unborn child enclosed in the womb. As they approach the men the drums swell to thunder and, three times, the women with the girl encircle the men and drums. They come to the seclusion hut with a crescendo of triumphant singing.

The instructress enters backwards, putting the girl down at the far side. That is so that the girl shall not look up and see the significant crutch of *mudyi* poles. She, hedged about by taboos to guard against infertility, frigidity, witchcraft, may not look up during the whole period of her seclusion. But mercifully and at last she can eat, though only after a sequence of symbolic gestures which she must find hardly endurable. The instructress cats a little of the food first, then the girl must put dabs of the cassava mush on various places—on the left *mudyi* pole, then on the right, and then she must take off all of such scant clothing as she wears—she must be naked. The bridegroom enters to light a fire which signifies marriage, and if well lit, augurs a successful marriage. During the lighting she must cover her eyes.

After eating she must have medicine to heighten her fertility; and, now, it is time for her handmaid to be brought to her, a small girl not yet old enough for initiation. Then the novice can go to her sleeping mat.

She goes to bed, but no one else. There is the night dance of

Kwing'ija, and that, though formally based, is roisterous. The day has accumulated a preoccupation with sexuality, particularly lauding its informalities. The women especially have been up-lifted, very ready now to lure lovers into the bush; they are the more fulfilled by the resultant quarrels, and often fights, between husbands and lovers. The dance goes on till dawn.

For the novice enclosed in her web of taboos in the seclusion hut there are no relaxations. There she must stay, looking down, clenched hands pressed to her temples, maintaining an attitude of modesty. She may not sing, talk loudly, or laugh. She must be obedient, not bold, not angry. Such food as is brought to her she must eat so that she may be fat and beautiful for her coming-out dance. She may not have anything to do with the fire; she may not cook or look at food as it is brought. There are other taboos. To break any would mean the ending of her *Nkang'a*, the loss of her marriage.

The seclusion period is for instruction, mainly in ritual dances and sexual techniques. Her teachers are her instructress and women helpers, who must teach her well. At *Kwidisha*, her coming-out, she must perform her dances faultlessly before the assembly of all the people.

For the dances she is dressed with a cloth passed between her legs, taken under her waist string, and draped before and behind like a skirt. She wears rattles at the small of her back and on her calves, and above the waist wears nothing.

Some of the dances mime the things of daily life—the masculine gathering of wild bees' honey, the catching of fish, sweeping, hunting. Some, such as *Chimbayeka*, are sexually stimulating. That has fast movement, a rapid stamping which agitates the rattles and makes a shaking of the breasts. She also learns the 'Dance of the Bed'. That is a highly realistic miming of the sexual act which ends with a lolling back of the head and a rolling of the eyes that caricatures the final state of the man.

There is intense emphasis that the first night of marriage shall have successful consummation—that relating to the obsessional theme of fertility—and much of the seclusion teaching is to make the girl sexually adept and physically ready. The instructress enlarges her vagina, simulating with a peeled sweet potato or cassava root made phallus-shaped. On either side of the navel and below it cicatrices are made because they are believed to have a tactile erotic effect.

This is in contrast to the ways of at least some other tribes, certainly of the Bemba. They attach great importance to the bride's affect of virginity, often, after the first night, telling with relish how long a difficulty they had. There is a quite brisk trade in the manipulative reconstruction of the affect of virginity. 'It's done by folding,' said a Bemba friend.

Kwidisha, the coming-out, begins after sunset on the last day of seclusion. The bridegroom's party arrives bearing gifts of cassava and calabashes of beer. The bride's party, with beer and cassava too, meet them to enact a ceremonial exchange. Men of both sides meet in a 'push of war' with much advance taunting as to the feeble strength of the other party. If, in the pushing, the bridegroom's party is master, the bride's mother and relatives are elated. Their girl is marrying into a strong race of men. This night, or perhaps later, the marriage payment is made.

Then, with night, the drums begin. The fire blazes, the dancing starts, and till dawn the night is lusty with dancing, adulterous fun and fighting.

At dawn they come to the girl in the seclusion hut. She lies awaiting them, head on hand, and at their coming performs the 'Dance of the Bed'. She sings, praises the new day. Then under her blanket she is led away. In the bush, screened by an ant hill, she is prepared. She sits quietly, clenched hands to her temples. About her neck they hang an amulet which contains medicine against her shyness, and then they prepare to dress her. They put

53

on her back rattles and her leg rattles and they dress her hair. It is combed and plaited and the instructress sings the circumcision song. Then altogether they sing the plaiting song and more songs after. Now, still naked otherwise, she is washed. So, concurrently, is her handmaid.

She is hung with strings of beads, looped round her neck and over her breasts; she is rubbed all over first with castor oil, then with red earth. White beads are put on her hair because white stands for fertility and the proper order of things in society. A caking of oil and red earth is put over the beads so that they lie secretly beneath. The handmaid is also rubbed with oil and red earth. The novice stands and a rolled cloth is put on, girdling her and another put between her legs and under the girdle to hang back and front. Through all she stands quietly with bowed head, modest downcast eyes, clenched hands to her temples.

Food is brought, cassava and chicken, and the girl, kneeling and sitting on her heels, is fed by hand by the instructress. With the meal done and she still downcast, she is painted on the forehead with rings of white clay. She is ready. She is about to come out.

Coming to the dancing place of the village she is screened from sight, skirting the village, a blanket held about her, because no one but her attendants may see her until her ceremony of entry. At the dancing place the drums are ready; the people are gathered and the headman sits on his stool by the drums.

The instructress and the handmaid go before, and at their coming the people sing. Then, at the coming into sight of the novice and her attendants, handmaid and instructress dance to meet her.

The blanket is snatched away. She is revealed. Then she, her handmaid, the instructress, the three together, dance into the circle of people. She dances crouching to the drums and touches them, then straightens up. The headman gives her his switch, which is his insignia. With her handmaid she kneels, then dances before the drums, leaps across the circle and back to the drums. She spits before them in blessing.

Now, till noon, she dances. She dances all the repertoire learnt in seclusion, beginning with the stamping dance, the *Chimbayeka*, and gifts are given as she dances. She does the fishing dance and the hunting dance and the others. Then with noon come she goes with the instructress to eat and rest till night and union with her husband.

Perhaps she is apprehensive about the coming of that; her bridegroom must be more so. The night will be the test of his virility. Not only the bride but all the people await the proof of that. Whatever the privacy of the marriage hut, the critical eyes of the village and the district are upon him. He goes with friends and the witch doctor into the bush where, while the bride rests, they ply him with aphrodisiac medicines. No possible stimulus is left unused. He is given medicines to drink and others are injected into that which must take the brunt of what is to come.

Evening comes and he goes to the hut to await the bride. He must sit bent, with an air of modesty. The instructress brings the bride; she carries her in backwards so that she shall not face the door and so become barren. Now he must stand, thus not to be flaccid. The handmaid comes too, but not to stay. The instructress thrusts two arrows into the ground, one each side of the bed. Now, she tells them, they are on their own. All that may be done for them is done. She leaves them.

Now it is the husband's duty to show the frontier of his stamina. He must show how high a count he can achieve—knowing that that is for the record. For this first night that must be all his business, with no divergencies of amorous play.

Before first light the instructress is back. She does knock, entering only upon the husband's permission. Her questioning eye fixes the bride. She, if all has been well, nods. The instructress shakes both by the hand, gives them water for washing and, leaving them, steals through the village throwing a morsel of black mud into each doorway. It is a symbol of love in the new marriage, and she brings a little of it to all in the community.

She comes again to them the next night, but only to tell them that she will leave them in peace to be as they will.

5

It was midday when we finished the round of the hospital. We were very hungry; we had not eaten since the meal with Chief Ikelengi the day before yesterday—the gnaw had accumulated. I thought Miss Wentworth eyed us searchingly.

'Would you care to come to my house for a cup of tea?

'Ah—you would. Come along then.'

Her sitting-room was bright and airy, with chintz curtains. We sank into armchairs and sighed. 'Tea!' said Kay. Miss Wentworth came soon with the tray—thin cups, fresh hot tea—as we drank, like hungry cats given milk, she watched.

'Are you hungry?' she asked suddenly.

We admitted it. When had we last eaten, she asked and, when we told her, got up purposefully.

'Better be eggs—take too long for anything more elaborate—won't take long. That'll do you good quickly.'

Soon, though it seemed like a long corridor of time, she returned with two eggs for each of us, and bread and butter. I wondered if it was worth fasting to find food so sublimely good. Not fasting *that* long, I decided as the pangs eased.

We were about to take our grateful leave when another woman came in—our lady of the bicycle of that other hungry day, real now and not in the least hallucinatory.

We went slowly back to Ikelengi, pausing in the villages to pass the time of day and restraining George between them. 'Don't you dare George,' we said when we saw women or chicken ahead.

In one village a man was building himself a house. He had spent his working life in the Copper Belt and now, elderly, well off in his terms, had returned for retirement to his native village. The house was half-built, the walls of sun-brick up, the roof poles of *muKwa* being thatched with grass. He passed a lingeringly possessive hand over the surfaces as he showed us. I had run out of matches and, from a secret place, he produced a box. He gave them, and I received them, with a little ceremony.

The next day, to be our last in the source country, we were to go to the Angolan frontier. There the Zambezi passes due west into Angola, then soon makes a turn due south till, far away, it flows again into Zambia. At the place of the exit from Zambia the frontier runs north and south, and north of the Zambezi the frontier is a tributary, the little Jimbe River. Close to it there is a frontier post.

There would be no time to walk because we must, that same night, return to Mwinilunga. We would take the truck and ask some from Ikelengi to come too for the ride.

Some of the men came and one of the women, a bouncing bonny strapping little person. She had an air, with her upflung head and horizontal thrust of bosom and buttocks. She could not for very long at any time restrain her huge smiles and sudden torrents of slightly hoarse speech.

We, Kay and I, rode in the cab with George. The others clung as they could in the empty rear, some on the sides and some on the naked sun-roasted metal floor. I was surprised no one was lost or injured—George hurled his truck as heedlessly as always and the road was rough.

It was highest heat of afternoon when we came to the frontier post. The molten air was white with heat and, in the white wooden building, it was stifling. Perhaps, when we had identified ourselves, that was a part cause of the men manning it volunteering to conduct us down to the river frontier, though anyway they were courteous and friendly men.

All together we went down in a fierce trap of heat, slowly because every movement enhanced the gout of sweat. Then there was the river, only about thirty yards across but looking so coolly, cravingly, watery. We sat on the bank, all of us, held down by the weight of sun and looking at that seduction of water. Nobody actually suggested it. I think one of the men stood up and began to peel off his shirt. Nobody said anything. We all stood up, stripped to the minimum of underwear, then plunged. We swam, floated, paddled, came out to dry on the bank then, as the sun began to tyrannize again, plunged again. Threat of evening finally drove us out of the water.

We had left it late and the light was thinning when we reached Ikelengi. We had not wanted to return to Mwinilunga after dark, but to ensure it the truck fell into one of its sudden deaths and this one looked more than usually final. But we were schooled. We waited fatalistically.

We waited and the air changed. Small whiffles of wind came recurrently stirring through the leaves and brushing chills on our faces. As the short twilight sank into night a purple-black shroud filled the whole sky. The lightning began as brief staccato flashes down the distant sky. But it augmented quickly, it and the thunder striding the miles till the shivering brilliance lit everything. The thunder towered and rolled in mountains of sound and our skulls seemed to yield and open under its pressure. There was no rain yet. The wind came in shrill gusts pressing like giant hands.

We were restive now. Come what may we must go to Mwinilunga. In the morning an aeroplane was to pick us up, and rainy season storms can make drastic havoc with bush roads. We remembered also that there were rivers to cross, and the bridges were simple things, just laid planks with no guarding rails, always precarious. If the storm should bring great rain, how would the rivers be? There were three of them, minor streams, but the smallest can become ferocious when storms come. Half an hour's delay might be the last half-hour of road and rivers being passable.

We did not push George, fiddling obscurely under the bonnet. We must not fluster him. We waited and fretted. When the engine did burst suddenly into rackety life we were relieved but not confident. The rain must come. For how long, how dependably would that truck stay mobile?

The rain began as we started. The huge sploshing drops fell separately. They increased and coalesced and became a solidity of water. With the rain the storm rose to frenzy, bursting the air. Lightning tore the night with eerie lucidities of light. At first moments of black totality punctuated the sheer brilliances. Then the intervals were cancelled and the whole world crouched under a continuous blue-white shiver. Blinding tongues plunged to earth round the entire night's circumference.

We might have thought that even George would have been awed into care but he flung the truck confidently and blindly into the maelstrom.

'George,' we shouted, 'George—drive more slowly.'

He went as wildly, heedless as the truck slewed in the disintegrating road.

'George—look out—George—there'll be floods. *Drive more slowly.*'

Then we hurtled sickly round a bend and the road was a lake. Impact for a moment quenched the thunder's roar. The truck careened and the displaced wall of water dropped on us like stone. George kept his foot down. Bucketing, skidding, we flung on behind a wave that shut out vision.

Incredibly we came out at the end of the flood. We turned on George.

'George! George!—lucky the engine isn't flooded—for God's sake man—slow down.'

He was smiling. The road surface was breaking up. The soft skin of dust had gone and the prongs of rain were prising through the stones. The floods came oftener and deeper and George charged them as if to kill them.

The windscreen wipers stopped. George attacked the brakes. In the pale blue fire and the thunder we lay in the water. It was over the hub caps. George got out and lifted the bonnet. He had his heavy spanner and applied it crushingly. That, curiously, was therapeutic. When he climbed back the wipers worked.

We roared on, and soon, into another flood. The engine stopped. 'That's it,' I shouted in Kay's ear. 'He's flooded the engine.'

George was still smiling. He climbed down again with his spanner to rain blows under the bonnet. Then he came back and the engine started. An unreasonable providence helps him, I thought.

Now, where the road was above water it was awash with little hold for a careful driver. With George we skated sickeningly, losing grip, regaining it, losing it again. The onrush of each wayside tree was a crisis, each sighing relief on passing quenched by the next.

Then the road dipped from under us. We saw it dropping to the first river, saw that the surface was gone, nothing left but a slide of sludge. We saw the swollen boil of river. George, snatched at last by panic, jammed on the brakes.

We began to slide, dropping on the slope, sliding and accelerating, this way and that, hurrying into a plunge. George wrestled with the disassociated wheel. We were lurching headlong and askew to the river. In chill clarity I saw the bridge's narrow span veering from us. We flew into a final sidelong slew, leaving the road, over its rotted shoulder. We were jammed in the cab without a chance of movement.

Then there was the water. As the spray of impact flew up we shuddered and flung into another skid. We sloped sideways and diagonally up from the river and over the shoulder, half sideways on to the railless bridge. We slithered across, from side to side, feeling the looseness of a wheel over the edge one side then the other. We came off sideways, swung about, zig-zagged up the slope with unspent impetus. We breasted the rise, straightened, regained purchase.

I suppose there was a rock in the margin of the water, just miraculously there for us to hit with velocity enough to give us that saving trajectory. The same unreasonable providence.

Now safe, the rigidity left like the air from a stabbed tyre. George, at last, was sobered. We added to that with fervent and unbidden words.

He drove soberly now, at least in his terms. But George was no man to dwell upon shocks. As his spirit lifted his foot went down. But the salutary residue was there—we shouted and he heeded. It was enough to give us the crossing of the other two rivers with no more than inescapable risk.

With the last river crossed in little more than the passing of a few breaths, the fury drained from the storm. The lightning died, the rain stopped. The peace was as unreal as the storm's nightmare. I suppose we were numbed. George seemed to have forgotten. He needed our pressure.

The worst of the road was passed. Nearer to Mwinilunga the floods decreased; the road had some remainder of surface. With searing relief we came to the outskirts. We had been just two hours coming from Ikelengi. It had been eternity.

We slept that night at the rest house. In the morning when I went out the world was wonderful. It was early, just after five, the air thin and clear, cooled and cleared by the storm. So it may be after the rainy season's early deluges, with the mornings washed to a paradisic clarity. From the terraced eminence of the rest house I could see to crystalline distances over the forest of the source country and beyond to the Congo. I sat on a low wall at the terrace's edge over the abrupt drop to the forest. The sensuous sweetness of frangipani hung on the air.

I turned when I heard someone come out of the rest house. It was Chief Ikelengi. He too had slept at the rest house. He was on his way to attend a meeting of the Council of Chiefs in Lusaka. We sat together on the wall and talked contentedly.

When George came with his truck to take us to the airstrip we allowed so generously for their joint unreliability that we were early, with an hour to wait before our aeroplane would come. There was the same vast emptiness that we had left, the same heat because it was mid-morning now. The same kites still wheeled against the burning sky and, surely, the same eagle tiny with altitude. Cicadas shrilled, lizards scudded, and there was no sound or movement of anything else. Under the sun I picked among the stones because stony ground in Africa should not be ignored. Semi-precious stones may lie among the others and airstrips are good places.

Then there was the distant drone. The speck against the sky enlarged and became an aeroplane, then landed. A white nurse had come with it. She was shepherding a very old man who was sick and was a chief and on his way to hospital. She helped his frail steps from the aeroplane, taking his weight.

'Come on, Chiefy, mind the step,' she said. 'You can do it. Now come along, Chiefy, don't worry, I've got you.'

She turned to us—'I've got to get poor old Chiefy into Mwinilunga—no transport seems to have turned up. D'you think I could have your truck?'

Of course, we said and told George to help them into the cab. He looked at the ground, smiling in the way we knew. He shook his head.

'Why won't you?' Kay asked, and he should have been warned by her tone. He said he did not want to. When Kay had finished he went wordless and submissive to help and drive them away. George, to the end, was George.

6

The frontier was at Lingelengenda. It had the strange air that frontiers often have. Immediately to the north, beyond the high wire fence, was Angola. Out of Angola came the Zambezi, far from where we had left it in the source country. In that interval it had grown to a large river.

A flagstaff carried the flag of Zambia; under it was a small building, white walled, starkly practical. There were bullet holes in the walls. Sometimes, the frontier officers said, there was shooting 'over there'. Bullets were no respecters of frontiers. A youth, sixteen perhaps or less, sat on a bench inside. He was under arrest.

'He came over the frontier,' they said.

We stood straining our eyes over the frontier, thinking of the bullets. But there was no shooting then, no alarm. The whole place under the still hot sky was empty, as if no life had ever been, with the significant-seeming emptiness that frontiers often have.

I was the more conscious of the things of territory, because we had left the river among the Ndembu and this was Luvale country. Though they do come from the same roots and by the same migration 300 years ago, the link is tenuous today. They have cultural ties still, with a similarity of customs and rituals—Luvale doctors may even officiate at Ndembu rites. But their sense of difference is sharp. Kay had had a friend, a Ndembu girl, and Kay, by a slip, once called her Luvale. For weeks thereafter she would not speak to Kay.

*A 'witch' at the
Kalere Hill Mission*

Ndembu woman, North Western Province

There is a story of how the great migration happened—and it, incidentally, gave more tribes to Zambia than just those two. It was so that the Bemba people came, the largest tribe in Zambia, and the Chokwe, Lwena, Luchazi and Songa. The father of them all, the great Chief Mwantiyanvwa, ordained that his people should build a tower to reach the sky so that they could bring him the moon and the sun. They strove and built high but, at last, the tower fell. Many people died in its fall. Hearing the story and how the people's fear of the great chief's anger was so intense that they fled, so beginning the migration, I remembered the fearful respect Chief Ikelengi's people had for him.

The river broadens abruptly at Lingelengenda, hard to believe as the same stream as the one of the forest against the Congo. We came down from the frontier, following the river through country clumped with high umbrella-topped columnar trees and under them villages as embowered as those of the Mwinilunga District, thicketed with banana, mango, pawpaw.

The river comes dramatically to Chavuma. The flow, distant between the banks till then, is constricted abruptly by a wall of jagged rock piled from both banks to leave at the middle a narrow throat. Through that goes the whole pent force of the river. The sound is unmistakably like the name *Chavuma*, and that, I had been told, was its origin. Kay was sceptical. The word, she said, had a precise meaning—'to blow' or something close to that. That was apt enough.

Otherwise the river had carved deeply; the land scarps up steeply from the water. Chavuma, on the edge of the plateau level, is high above the water. It was odd that a force that had trenched so deeply into rock, itself so hard, had cut so small a breach in the barrier. We stood at a precipitous point above the river; the ground dropped from our feet in a conglomerate of rock, huge blocks, boulders, small stones, that fell down the face. Under the drop lay a great bay in a wide white brilliant sweep of sand. A sepia swarm of naked children played there with distant treble shrieks.

I do not remember how we came to the American mission but there we were that morning, strangers. The door opened and we were absorbed.

I come to missions dubiously; I am conscious of a need, as it seems to me, for some missionaries (like some other religious professionals) to maintain a constant appearance of 'goodness'. Come what may they must upon the instant stiffen the upper lip which is ready to confess the normal human weaknesses from which they have no exemption. It makes them suspect. It becomes hard to credit them with ordinary earthy genuineness.

So, coming into the mission at Chavuma, for the first minutes and longer I could not trust my instinctive response. We were so gently received, kindly and warmly. There were four, two men, Philip and Tom (or so I will call them) who had married each other's sisters. The house was wholly American, gay, neat, airily clean, with bright rugs on a polished floor, frilled curtains and china on the shelves. Beyond the window the panorama of bush and river was there to remind me that I was in Africa.

I felt self-consciously bush-soiled. 'But don't worry,' they said, and pushed us to an immaculate flowered sofa. 'What's a bit of honest bush dirt? Why don't you just sit there and we'll get some coffee? I guess that'll keep you going until lunch comes up.'

Come up it did, soon, tranquil and orderly, and with the blessed luxury of that and the easy conversation, I began to forget that these kindly people were missionaries. But, I prompted myself, they *are*, and how easy it is to be stiffly opinionated about missionaries. Too often in even casual conversation with the religiously dedicated there is the apprehensive sense of skating constantly close to their piety, and that inhibits conversation. These were sanguinely pleasant people who happened to be missionaries.

I suppose they were a modern humanly sophisticated generation, in a way their forerunners were not. We were joined at lunch by the mother of one of the men; she was of the old kind.

'Let me tell you,' she said suddenly to me, out of her silence till then, 'let me tell you how my children came to God.'

It was a rather long story, circumstantial. 'My little child was only five and she came to me, that little child and she said, "Mummy, take me to God, I want to be saved", and I took her to the good Lord.'

Her son and daughter waited politely, but when they could steered conversation elsewhere.

'We'll expect you to dinner,' they said after lunch and then took us to the two bungalows where we were to sleep. They, wonderfully, had a sitting-room softly done out with cushions and sofas and lamps and beyond, a soft bed and a bathroom. I tried each easy chair and the sofa, then the bed.

We went to dinner and it was memorable. Now there were just Philip and Tom and their wives; they melted the last of my reservations. The evening became mellow.

'Yes,' Tom said, 'this *is* Luvale country but there are a whole lot of Lunda here too—the mixing isn't all that equable. They're often at loggerheads—pretty often it's quite violent loggerheads.

'They come in from all round to our hospital here, for every sort of thing—you remember, Philip, the lady from across the river—she was Luvale, wasn't she—who came for pre-natal treatment? Now she was, you see, in medical terms a psycho-ceramic —a crackpot. It was part of her peculiarity that she wouldn't take medicines from an African—they must come to her from white hands—and often. Every fifteen minutes, night and day, she'd come knocking at the door asking for drugs. It really did become a bit of a bother. But she was cured—inadvertently.

'We had a pet baboon, a big fellow, and once in every day we'd let it loose for play—it was playmates with the dogs. Those games were boisterous, with a whole lot of huge tumbling and play ferocity. Well, they were playing one day when the lady from across the river came calling. Just as she's there, there's this baboon hurtling round the corner of the house in flight from the dogs-- and she didn't see the dogs. She just saw this baboon. I guess it seemed to be coming straight at her.

'Burdened as she was, she was up the path to the road in one bound and up the road—you saw it's a steep incline, didn't you?— in a breath. She was last seen breasting the top with daylight under both feet. She went straight to the hospital and, 'straight away, she had her baby with no trouble at all. The whole thing seemed to do her good—it was salutary. No more trouble with her at all—completely normal after that.

'She wasn't a psycho-ceramic any more—you see she hadn't been *zalukia*—mental, really gone, you know—just *matachi*, temporarily mental.'

We got to talking of snakes, as is the way in Africa, and, though you see them so little if you are mobile, even walking the bush, staying in one place the presence is there, constantly. They come into houses.

'There was a time,' one of the girls said, 'when one of the dogs, a bitch, had puppies and—you know how children are with puppies—our little boy Danny went to see them. Right away I heard the bitch growling fiercely—and you know that was so unexpected from that gentle dog that I went hurriedly to see. There was a python, ten feet long or more—it had already eaten three puppies—and the dog was between it and Danny, growling, warning him to keep away.

'We killed the snake. We opened it, got the puppies out. They were dead.'

'There was that evening too, d'you remember,' Philip's sister said, 'when our little girl was put to bed and the door of her room became locked on the inside. I went round to the back of the

68

house and from there through another door and into the bedroom. It was dark and I had to feel my way across to the locked door. As I was unlocking it I felt a splash on the side of my face—I yelled to ask who was spraying me—as if anyone could with me shut in the room, but I guess I was taken aback. Then I got the door open and, do you know, there right at my feet was this spitting cobra. Just very narrowly the venom had missed my eyes.'

Spitting cobras are two of the various species of African cobra—ringhals cobra and black-necked cobra; both spit, or, more accurately, squirt their venom. They do it with impressive range and accuracy—the jet goes arrow-straight to its target six or seven feet away. The target is invariably the face, particularly the eyes and, reaching there, it penetrates the delicate veins. Stories of the effect of that are horrific but the blindness it causes is temporary. Two days is average. Otherwise, unless the venom reaches a cut or abrasion it is harmless. Ordinarily a spitting cobra is a spitter, but pushed enough it will use its fangs, without the lethal result of other cobras. The victim is very unpleasantly ill, but lives.

We went for breakfast next morning to Tom's house, close to Philip's. The early sun streaming into the kitchen-breakfast room caught the long fair hair of Tom's daughter. At a guess she was eleven or twelve, demure, gently old-fashioned; in her flowered calf-length dress, she reminded me of Alice. As became her as hostess she talked to us gravely, smiling quietly and showing us her pet bush baby.

We ate waffles and maple syrup with American coffee at the gaily clothed table by the window—beyond the window and below us lay the broad river with towering *matete* grass and wild banana forests at its margin and Africans, purple-black in the sun, poling dug-out canoes. The river there was dangerous with crocodiles.

Balovale, eighty miles downstream, was our next objective,

and in that interim just bush thinly scattered with villages—no rest houses, little expectation of finding food. We had no bearers and so could carry no camping gear or food.

'Why don't you,' said Tom, 'walk the country downstream for a couple of days? I'll come before sundown each day with the boat to find you. After that I'll take you by river down to Balovale.'

We went down through the villages that first day, threading the bush from one cluster of conical thatched huts to the next and at each the children came curiously to stare at us. We went desultorily, with no sense of form—shape and time and direction are neutralized in such vastness of space. There was a sense that we could go through an infinity of such sun-blinded days with the same blue vault forever dropping to horizons never reached, with an identical succession of clearings with huts crouching for shade under the bananas and mangoes. On tracks between villages we met old men walking with bows and arrows.

We did come to a larger village and that had a still. In the arched shade of a banana clump where the swords of sunlight thrust as little as possible, it was distilling *kachipembe*. Three people had charge of it—a boy about eleven, a woman who leaned with sun-drowsed eyes against a banana stem and, sitting in the dust, a woman with her baby. Chicken scratched the dust and fishing baskets made a partial enclosure. How long the distilling of *kachipembe* takes I do not know; these three were not counting the hours.

The raw material may be maize beer or it may be mixed fermented fruits and vegetables in water. It goes in a large gourd over a fire in a loose hearth of stones. A pipe goes from the gourd through a trough hewn from a baulk of timber and in the trough is water for cooling. Under the end of the pipe where it emerges from the trough a bottle stands to receive the condensed spirit coming drip by drip. The bottle of this still was two-thirds full of the colourless and slightly cloudy liquid. The stuff has a fearsome reputation—evil and scarifying, it is said to be, burning the wits out of its victims in the end.

The three attending it there seemed far from that end. The pipe dripped, the sweating minutes hung, passed slowly and, very slowly, the bottle filled. The three watched in bottomless placidity. It was a leisurely road to ruin.

We walked by the river next day and we would have covered more miles than we did but for the stones. There was a place a few miles downstream of Chavuma where the scree of stones was heaped up from the water to the plateau's high level above, and if you are subject to the fascination of stones, such a thing cannot be passed. The river runs in igneous and metamorphic rock and that can yield treasure. The Zambezi's bed and marginal spoil has many semi-precious stones—agate, carnelian, malachite, garnet, rose quartz, amethyst, and others. The really lucky—or less ignorant—searcher *may* find precious ones too. I never have. You need to be able to recognize them.

We found none then. Most of the stones, from little nodules up to slabs, had a curiously soapy texture, mostly warm green, with an outer skin. It suggested the skin of a cheese. The smooth inner surfaces were pleasant to the fingers and we sat among them feeling them and conjecturing the sensuous results of shaping and polishing. It was frustrating not to be able to identify them.

The miles were lonely below Chavuma. Walking fast, scrabbling, leaping flood-torn gulleys down sand slopes—the miles accumulated and we saw not a soul nor a hut nor any human sign. The going was rough and sometimes painful; so many pretty plants are vicious. The *matete* reed, which is a form of *Phragmites*, stands high and lovely and makes stately thickets by the water. It looks as innocent as water plant can be but every leaf that climbs its stem is a spear—needle-sharp and piercing at a touch. There is a dwarf acacia which crouches low with a downily modest prettiness. The delicate web of its little leaves on the mazey twigs is fairy-fine; but set closely up every twig are curved and spiteful spines. Their least, but multiple, touch makes a bleeding laceration. All the care that experience breeds never protects fully.

We walked fast but circumspectly. The next day we must leave Chavuma and how could we hope again for such hospitality? Perhaps, down-river, we would find food but I must hunt for it if the chance came. We came cat-like to every clump of cover or undercut of bank. There was cause for caution anyway.

You can come upon crocodiles very unexpectedly. They have been stringently put down, greatly thinned where formerly they teemed, but it is foolhardy to assume their absence. Upstream a few miles from Livingstone there is a boat club, much frequented. But it was there, drinking on its verandah, that I heard of a young man who swam, right by the mooring stage. He was seized by an unsuspected crocodile. Someone dived to help him but that was the last of him.

It is easy not to see a crocodile, as I learnt once, though I was lucky. That was not on the Zambezi but its tributary the Kafue River, in an area away from bush tracks, uninhabited. There was a lagoon which, out of the rainy season, was separated from the river; I thought it looked worth fishing. I recall that, approaching it, it was necessary to make a detour. In the etched shade of a thorn tree there was a pride of lions—the lion, the lioness, three cubs—resting out the day's heat.

There was a need for prudence anyway. A hippo occupied the lagoon. As hippos will it submerged from time to time, then emerged with the vast explosive sigh that signifies the whole wet bliss of water under the sun of noon. There is no more peaceful sound; it is soporific, but it should not deceive you. Hippos are odd tempered. Nothing ruffles them more than trespass upon their sense of territory. Give no suggestion of invasion and, mostly, they will treat you distantly, with sleepy disinterest. But go upon the water in a boat, or, on land, between them and the water and they resent it.

This one, in the restriction of the lagoon, thought any approach an infringement. As I approached it moved shoreward. Then, hove-to just offshore, it fixed me with pink-rimmed eyes and rumbled discouragement. I fished but, moving along the bank, kept a measuring eye on the hippo. Then I saw the crocodile, just its eyes; that is all you do see.

They lie just sub-surface and their eyes, which are elevated from the skull, are just above the surface. They are unfriendly eyes. But this one was quite well out. I thought we would not bother each other. I continued to fish my slow way round the bank. I forgot the crocodile.

I reached the further side of the lagoon, still shadowed by the hippo. The grass was dense there, waist high; I should have remembered that high grass can conceal many things. But I was fishing and that breeds forgetfulness. I pressed through. Then I stubbed my foot.

Ground and grass and everything erupted. The heavy thrash that swept close to my legs was, as I glimpsed, the tail of a crocodile. I saw no more than that and it had gone, sliding into the water. It must have been sleeping there. I was glad that it was its tail I stubbed, not its head.

I came to a rock and sat to light my pipe, as composure returned, I looked down. Between my feet was the latter half of the cast skin of a cobra. The forward half disappeared into a snake-sized hole under my rock. In the same moment I perceived that the hippo, now out of patience, was advancing purposefully. It had begun to seem unsafe; I left.

A game warden told me of his experience with a hippo close to that same place. This one was a rogue hippo, a solitary too vile tempered to live with its kind. It was its habit to rush in violent attack upon anything that passed near. Since once in a while men came fishing that way it was necessary that he should remove the danger. It was as he and I fished at the place that he told me the story. A hundred yards or so across the river at the tail of an island a party of hippo wallowed with huge sleepy sighs. It was as peaceful a sound as summer cattle in an English meadow.

'There was no peace with that one,' he said, and told me how he had come stealthily with his rifle, creeping up the river in a boat not far out from the bank.

'I had just come opposite that clump of *matete* when it burst open. Before I could do a thing that great mad hunk of hippo was on me. He turned the boat over and I suppose that saved me. I dived and swam under water—if I could stay under long enough perhaps I could get to the bank without his seeing me. I expect I could have done but that damn beast came thrashing about trying to find me. He didn't, but one of his forefeet caught my arm— stripped the flesh from shoulder to elbow and shattered the bone. Don't know how I got out of the water really. Was in hospital for three months.

'I bet you can guess the first thing I did when I came out—I went straight back with a rifle and that time I got him.'

Now, going down from Chavuma, we saw no crocodiles, though we saw plenty of their tracks. They are unmistakable— the double print of the feet and the central trough in the soft sand made by the drag of tail. I thought it a reassuring sign—though to find it so depends upon an objectivity hard to maintain if you live in daily and lifelong proximity to crocodiles. The people of the riverside villages have lived in cold dread of them—too often women fetching water have been seized, seen no more. Men in their unstable dugout canoes have been too often fatally vulnerable. They hated crocodiles, waged relentless war against them. Probably that would not have been decimating but to it was added the steady, and deadly, activity of professional crocodile

74

hunters. They traded in the skins. Crocodiles had been thinned disastrously. To the people of the villages it seemed no disaster but a blessing—but the knocking of such large holes through any ecology has repercussions. The fishing, upon which they depended dearly, suffered. Many crocodiles eating many fish means large well-nourished survivors. Few crocodiles eating few fish means too many undersized under-nourished fish and, consequently, under-nourished villagers. It has as well disturbed the balance between tiger fish and their prey, the cichlid fishes, tilapia, and other kinds, which have the greatest importance as food. Too few tiger fish eaten by crocodile means too many tiger fish eating tilapia.

That is a good reason for protecting crocodile. There is another one: if we accept the need for conservation, which in sanity we must, it must be comprehensive, and include the perhaps not wholly agreeable crocodile and snake as well as the exquisite impala.

That does not imply that we and all the other species do not live competitively, balanced one against the other for the continuance of all. The greatest single key to the rhythm of life on earth is the equilibrium maintained between prey and predators, and man is one of the predators. He too kills to survive—but it is equally competitive individuals he was designed to kill, not whole species and whole environments.

By the will of Nature, man is instinctively a hunter. Natural conservation *depends* upon hunting, as long as it is in a natural frame. The fault is only in human factors which decimate mindlessly and indiscriminately. Because wildlife in the modern world has been so disastrously pinched, recreational hunting must be limited or, in some cases, stopped.

But the instinct remains, beyond entire suppression. I felt the nudge of it when a hunter told me, seducingly, of night hunting for crocodile. Why shouldn't we, he suggested, make a night foray on a part of the Zambezi that was 'crawling with croc'? I was tempted, and perhaps I would have fallen, but, the Game Department put its stern and proper ban on that expedition.

You go in a small boat; a torch is mounted on your rifle. By its beam you scan the bank as you steal down-river and I knew the sense of that. The night shrills and mutters, you hear grunts and sighs, the cavernous mumblings of hippo at unguessable proximities; the darkness is full of rustling threats and sudden sounds to bring a prickle to the scalp. Then the torch's beam picks up a reflecting gleam of red, two red glows. That is the eyes of a crocodile.

You stand in the bows with your rifle. The boat is eased in, silently and slowly. Then there is the crocodile, within reaching distance, captured by the light. Your heart thumps in your throat as you raise the rifle. You aim at the top of the head.

The shot may bring instant death with no subsequent movement; more probably reflex action will create a thrashing confusion. Now you must jump into the river. The instant action of a shot crocodile is to submerge and be lost. You must throw the grip of your arms round its jaws and acutely foolhardy as that sounds it would be more so but for a peculiarity of the crocodile. The clamp of its jaws to close is very powerful; the power for opening them is much less. So, your grip taken, you must keep it. With your companion in the water to hold the lash of the tail, you lug and struggle till the beast is on the bank. That, anyway, is what my hunter friend said. Since then, a former crocodile hunter has told me not to discount the crocodile's power to open its jaws—'It's powerful enough,' he said.

There is a total ban on the hunting of crocodile. Undoubtedly up and down the far miles of the river, where the distant rulings of the Game Department seem less urgent than the daily danger, crocodiles *are* killed. But the ban has a better than partial effect, enough to prevent the extinction of the species. The villagers'

76

odd killings, anyway, have never wrought the damage of systematic professional hunting. There had been sidelong suggestions in Chavuma that should I find a crocodile I should shoot it. But I sought edible game and it showed plentifully—out of range. Flights of duck and geese were constant up and down the river. So were hunters more mobile than I—yellow-billed kite were ubiquitous. Chicken hawk they call it there and they say it without love.

The fish eagle was hardly less common and it is a majestic bird, the national emblem of Zambia, a transcendent symbol. You can describe the parts—the snowy head and neck, the yellow cheeks and great scimitar of beak, the black spread of wings and the rich cinnamon of shoulders and underside, but that leaves untouched the true splendour of the creature. You see it on the highest branch above the river, an imperious silhouette. It throws back its head, opens the gape of its beak to the sky, and the wild loneliness of its cry is a moving sound. Then it drops to the water on its sweep of wings, beats there for a moment, then lifts, in its talons, a large fish.

The miles fell behind us and we had walked into the afternoon without coming into range of game. Then, in a great bend of the river where the margin of sand lay naked into the distance, a bunch of duck sat by the water. They were about half a mile away and there was not the smallest twig of cover. They looked inviolate.

Half a mile on the belly is a long way. I squirmed from hollow to hollow, pushing with feet and elbows, and sand under a tropical sun has the touch of the hot plate of a cooker. The range, at last, was narrowed to a hundred yards with not an inch of depression left. The shot killed two ducks.

'There's more than one meal,' Kay said, 'if we can eat them before they go off.'

7

Balovale I must call it because it was so I knew it. The name is changed now. Zambezi it is now called and however valid the reason I regret it. The old name had flavour and sense and meaning; there was the colour of the thing in it, and perhaps there is in the new name too but I don't know. I knew the old name and the sense of it.

That was the name because it is the heart and centre of the Luvale people's country—and indeed you can spell it *Baluvale* though *Balovale* is the common way. But the sense is the thing and that is that the prefix *Ba* is a plural, it renders plural that which it precedes. Thus *Baluvale* or *Balovale* is a plurality of the Luvale people—a free transcript is 'all the Luvale'. Though that *is* freely the meaning of it, it is misleading—Luvale country this is, they predominate through the Balovale District. But they are not 'all the Luvale'. The Luvale, it so happens, are one of the least territory-conscious of tribes, spread widely and apparently haphazardly. They occur all over North Western Province and in Western Province, Barotse country, there are almost as many as in North Western Province. So it is, but wherever else the Luvale may be Balovale has the spirit of them and is their centre. We left to go there in the morning as the sun climbed.

Tom kept his boat at the great sandy bay. We had to go there slowly from the mission because so many people were pressing that way. There was an excitement and nearer the river it quickened. We were nearly to the last level before the drop to the river when we came up on the women. They were going in single file, with a lilting shuffle matched to the beat of their singing, going slowly with a rolling of the belly which passed into a twitching quiver running down the legs and agitating the rattles. The rattles were a kind of coconut or something similar, tangerine-size, perforated and with a stone inside. They were in a double row down the backs of the legs and more were clustered in the small of the back against the bouncing buttocks. Also in the small of the back, worn in the fashion of a bustle, they had a big bundle of metal beer bottle tops threaded on strings so that they jingled with the movement. Their heads rolled on boneless necks and their faces were painted with white clay.

Among the trees at the lip of the drop to the river there was a ceremony. They were enacting the final part of *Mukanda*, the boys' circumcision ritual. In the centre of the circle of pounded and polished earth the *makishi* doctor was dancing, so skaken by the shudder of it that all his parts were disassociated. To the tips of his fingers and to his toes he was enveloped in a stocking-like garment, like knitted string, striped and patterned. Its impersonality and the huge beaded and painted mask gave him a preposterously superhuman seeming of significance. He was encircled by the women as he danced, running at them with monstrous and disarticulated miming of menace.

The women danced, leaning forward, straight-backed from the hips, bellies rolling and buttocks fluttering orgasmically. The rattles and beer top bustles jangled and they sang an insistent repetitive chant loudly and metallically. They appeared to be defying the *makishi*; his agitation grew to frenzy, matched by theirs.

There was another man among the dancers, a little one, in the same stockinged envelopment, with a smaller mask inclined upward and backward, fixed at the sky with a gaze of bliss. He shuffled shrugging and shuddering from part to part of the crowd of women, in each place gathering them in a long rectangle, seeming to harangue them and coax them. Particularly he attended the white-painted relatives of the boy novices.

Then he broke from them suddenly and, weaving and pointing, bore down on me. The absorbed heavenward stare of the mask gave him a queerly sinister look till I saw the gleam of his eyes and his smiling teeth in an opening in the neck of the mask.

'You have to give him a coin,' someone said, and when I did, he touched his hands together and swayed away.

I thought it unlikely that the *makishi* would allow me to take photographs and because I did not want to be caught doing it surreptitiously I produced my camera rather ostentatiously. Sublimated as the *makishi* was, he saw that. He halted, fell into a frenzy of trembling and pointed. Shouting, stabbing at me with shaking finger, he advanced on staccato-drumming feet. As he came, parting the shrilling women, they came too. I put my camera away. In the moment they seemed to forget me, dropping back into their ecstasies where they had left them.

That quickened now, rising to fever. The *makishi*, weaving in the enclosure of women, shook violently. Abruptly he stopped. He became rigid. Then as if a demon had taken him he leaped shouting at the women. They scattered like leaves, screaming with terror-starting eyes. He ignored them; he rushed to the edge where the ground dropped down through the bushes.

There he vanished. Two women followed him to the edge, stiffly bent forward from the waist, swaying with furiously shuffling feet, faces distorted with fury. They flung angry arms, screamed after him.

Now we went down to the beach to go, as we thought, to where Tom was already waiting at the boat. When we came to distant sight of him across the great sweep of sand we were checked. Near Tom in the flat white blaze of sun there was a small dark knot of men, with them the two boy novices. They saw us; one detached himself, rushing towards us shouting as he came, pointing. He looked curiously unlifelike, an agitated puppet dark against the burning light. We saw his face as he came nearer; it was twisted with fear and anger.

'Stop,' he was shouting, 'you must not come. It is bad. You must not come.'

He had stopped now, twenty yards from us, shaking and pointing. He pointed at me.

'You can come. But not the woman—not the woman!'

Then I remembered the *Nkanga* ritual of the girl novices among the Ndembu; I remembered its stringent taboos against a girl being seen by men before her coming-out dance—what dire things, barrenness, frigidity, other things, would overtake her upon the breaking of the taboos. It could be assumed that the *Mukanda* ritual was no less fearsomely beset with taboos. At the easiest guess impotence and infertility would be penalties.

So we were halted there so that no damning beam of Kay's eye should fall upon the boys—though she could not fail to see them as clearly, if distantly, as I could. And I thought what small tender things they looked even for merely ceremonial invitation into manhood. Their bodies, still childishly smooth and unmuscled, were naked except for a grass skirt. They stood timidly in the hot centre of the ceremony.

They were forming up now into a procession, the *makishi* at its head, the boys behind and behind them the others. They went slowly, from the water, to the foot of the slope which rose sharply to the dancing place above. There they stopped. There was more ritual now, the *makishi* incanting and dancing, the little boys so soon, unbelievably, to be men, standing meekly. Now a man went apart, up the slope a little way. He carried a gun. It was huge, a very old muzzle loader; when I saw he was going to fire it I feared for the safety of the thing. The shot came, softened in the hot distance, and at its signal they began to move up the slope.

Probably, as so often in male ceremonial, the gun had a hunting significance.

We waited as they made the ascent to the women above, loud and jubilant now, stamping and dancing and chorusing to accept the boys as men. I supposed this to be the equivalent of the final public coming-out of a girl in *Nkanga*. As with the girls, the boys would have been in seclusion till now, probably for a week, tied in a web of taboos and recovering from the wound of circumcision.

When we joined Tom at the boat he was enigmatic, as if he was purporting not to have seen what had passed. He made no comment, no reference at all. I wondered what he was thinking. There had been a confrontation of dogmas, each blessed with certainty.

We left then, starting the outboard engine, skirting the white boil of the river's burst through the rock throat, soon dropping downstream of all sight and sound of Chavuma. We had eighty river miles to go, all empty of human presence except for the three of us. The river was big now, often half a mile or more from bank to bank, the sun was hot and high, 103 degrees Fahrenheit by mid-morning and we were free of everything but the need for arrival.

We passed from the enormous privacy of one vista to another, an inconsequential human dot. The banks lay back, richly wooded, dropping to sandy strands blindingly white. Where the river turned often sand filled the inside of the turn for two or three miles, hot, white, blackly dotted with recurrent regiments of yellow-billed kites. There were islands, sometimes archipelagos, sandy mazes channelled by the river, forested with *matete*. In the dazzle of open spaces between, crocodiles lay like huge crenellated slugs. When we passed they slid their loggy bulk into the river with the ease of oil trickles, leaving hardly a ripple. What a frightful perfection they had, I thought watching them, what efficiency for stealing unsuspected upon a wading victim. You could step from the sand into those clear shallows and be grabbed with no warning at all.

I suppose no creature has a more evilly repellent look than a crocodile; it does so well express its lurking menace. In Nature's usual way of crossing purposes for ultimate efficiency the crocodile's aspect is a warning and an aid to the danger of it. The frightening reptilian yellow eye, the horrid jaws, convey the chilled threat of every awful thing that ever crawled or slid or grabbed from under dank and shadowed crevices. Nothing, summoning such old race memories, warns more than does the crocodile. But this is also the most perfect of camouflages. The victim is warned and the killer is hidden, lessened vulnerability balanced against heightened hunting competence.

Unquestionably, by normal standards the crocodile is ugly—most would say hideous and that, if the word is used in its pure sense, is true. The crocodile is hideous and it is horrid but not, with words truly used, ugly. Beauty is so much confused with what is pretty, attractive, winsome; ugliness is taken to be the contrary of that. But a skeleton has consummate beauty, of a kind that often parallels fitness for functioning. A crocodile is beautiful in the same context.

'Why don't we try for a tiger?' Tom said, and we moved in to cruise slowly near the shore—the advantageous place to try for a tiger fish. They haunt those cornery places of roots and rotting log piles, ferociously picketing to chop off the smaller fish which get a living there. There is a scale of pillage.

Tilapia feed there, and they are partially vegetarian. To prey on them there are their relatives, the so-called large-mouth bream. They engulf the tilapia, and the smaller tiger fish eat the smaller ones of both tilapia and large-mouth bream. The big tiger fish come to chop off the lives of all regardless. They, in their turn, fall victim to the crocodile. So it goes, round and round; all must live warily. Any that are the least bit less keen and well are the sacrificial ones that go to keep their species healthy and within bounds.

No creature is more unremittingly, raveningly malignant than a tiger fish and that is the means of catching it. You offer it, or pretend to offer it, living flesh. Because it is the commonest form of flesh in the tiger's world you offer fish flesh, though the tiger is as ready to accept any other kind. Steak is a deadly bait for tiger.

To simulate fish you use a device famous among those who pursue tiger fish in Central Africa—a spoon-shaped piece of burnished metal attached to a large hook forged flat for added strength—the Zambezi spoon. The hook is so formidable and the spoon so strong because anything less robust would be crushed by the armoured clamp of the tiger's jaws.

We had our Zambezi spoons. As the custom is we trailed them slowly close to the bank so that, flashing, fluttering, faltering, they should look like small fish lamed by injury. Such are first victims to the tiger fish.

Our fishing fortune was as it often is for tiger fishers—many tigers making smashing assault upon the spoon, few remaining attached. The violent wrench comes, you try in the moment to drive home the hook, and the tiger is in the air, flame and silver, a violent arc. Then, so often, you see the spoon fly from the fangy jaws. When, once in so many times, the hook takes and keeps a hold, it fastens you to the leaping frenzy of the fish until—at last—it is drawn to the boat balefully beautiful.

Its looks, like the crocodile's, declare its nature—but this is no skulker. It is brilliant, fierce, splendid, deep blue on the back, silver burnished on the flanks, fins flaring orange striped with black. The whole fish has a plated look, the big scales and faceted head striking back the light, contrasting with the black stripes that run from head to tail. Perhaps the stripes give it its name, perhaps its nature does; certainly its teeth could. They cram the jutting

84

jaws, projecting razor fangs that interlock, upper and lower, in a fixed grinning snarl. Tiger fish is the only possible name.

We caught them intermittently, with no great determination. The fishing was no more than a part of the lonely river day, partly an excuse for dawdling intimacy with the banks and the water. The birds went with us, tied by curiosity, particularly the kingfishers, the pied kingfisher and the great kingfisher, the one svelte, black and white, slim-looking for the stripes which run into the black beak, the other huge for a kingfisher, with a bristled head as if cut by a central European barber. They went ahead, the two of them, so far, forty yards or so, then waited till we came up, then ahead again. I hope they returned safely. They came miles with us.

We landed on an island for lunch. It sounds casual—an idling day on the river and home to tea. It was no casual thing that we *had* lunch, and if Tom had not brought it and hot coffee too we would not. And the island was no willow-shaded tie-up place for punts, no Thames eyot. It was aboriginal jungle that showed no sign of footfall before ours. We scrutinized it for crocodile and went ashore.

There was soft sand under a knotted vaulting of boughs, arching under the canopy to make a cavern of shade. When we had made sure there were no snakes we lay in the cool comfort to eat and watch the river through the curtain of aerial roots festooning the boughs.

But we had dawdled too long. There were many more miles before we could come to Balovale; the day was shortening and Tom must return that night. We tried no more for tiger. Tom opened the throttle. We surged through the enormous silences of the reaches, finding the channel and going at tangents to avoid sandbanks and reefs, trailing our wake and scaring the birds and disturbing the basking crocodile. We settled into something apparently endless—when a journey passes landmarks, buildings, recognizable chartable things, it has form, a beginning and an end. Here there was no changing form; we followed the bending river, out of one reach into another, beyond that another. There was no change, always the endless bush on either distant bank, the same hanging tangle of trees at the margins between the dazzle of the sandbanks, the kites and the eagles and the cranes rising ahead, the blank blue empty sky. We became torpid; we fell silent. Tom, in the stern, who had been before and knew landmarks, fixed the forward distance with searching eyes. He believed in arrival.

Though I had no comprehension of arrival I knew we would arrive and I was anxious. Night falls early, not long after six, and Tom had his way to make back up river, against the current. Night must come upon him so soon after leaving Balovale. I thought of the wild uncertainties of the river's bed, how tortuously you must find passage in daylight; and he would be tired. I thought of the crocodiles. I became eager for an end to the journey, willing it to come. But the distances unrolled and never a change, never a sign of humankind.

When Balovale did come it was unexpected. We came through a bend, cutting it near the bank, and there were people. They were women and naked children washing in the river under the high drop of the bank and waving to us. We passed them, completed our passage of the turn, and there was Balovale.

Tom would hardly give us time to thank him. He landed us, turned his bows upstream, opened the throttle. We watched until his wake turned the bend and distance smothered the sound. We heard later that he did arrive, late but safe. He had gone aground several times.

8

We walked up from the river, going slowly in the last of the hot
daylight, following the deep dust of the track that threaded under
the trees to Balovale. The town lay back from the river and to
call it a town is misleading. The whole place was parklike, randomly settled among the trees, a spacious shaded dapple under
the acacias and jacarandas and flamboyants—the jacarandas a lilac
torrent of blossom, the flamboyants a smother of the huge flame-
coloured flowers. We walked unburdened and at ease because we
had left our gear by the river to be brought up by men who had
met us there. The A.D.S., the Assistant District Secretary, had
been expecting us they said, and had sent them. If we would go to
the rest house he would find us. It was so that we were to meet
Joe. I can never think of Balovale, as it still was then, without
thinking of Joe.

The rest house was at the fringe of the place where Balovale
began to gather itself a bit as if trying to be a true town and less
of a beautiful idling of houses in the shade and the blossom. Just
close to where it consolidated enough to form itself into a centre
snuggling about the one brief broad street, there stood the rest
house, with its back to the centre, placidly facing the open acres
under the trees and a few steps from the airstrip. You could
almost, or so it seemed to me, have jumped from the street to the
airstrip, but perhaps I am remembering Balovale more impres-
sionistically than accurately. Perhaps there was more of it than I
remember, other streets, a denser settlement. But whatever the

detail of it my impression is true enough—the happy casualness with space, shady airy flowery tree-set space. Inconsequential tracks criss-crossed it and I could never guess the purposes of all the unhurrying scattering of people that seemed always to be using all the tracks.

As we came to the rest house that first evening a party of women and girls on one track and another party on another contrary track walked with fish baskets. *Ku swinga* they call that, 'to fish with a basket', and the baskets, about five feet long and the shape of a boat, are so light that the women carried them easily on their shoulders and over their heads like enormous hats. The smaller girls carried smaller baskets. We were looking at them when Joe came.

It was all official at first. Joe was an officer of the state and coming in his duty to receive us and that he did with correctness. But being Joe (as we so soon learnt), he could not have gone through the formula—his introduction of himself, his formal offer of such help as we might need, all that—without the jolly warmth and welling friendliness bubbling through.

He was energetic too. Had we brought food? He asked because it is the normal custom at rest houses to have a resident staff who will cook food brought by guests, though no food is supplied by a rest house. We had none and he rummaged and ferreted and chivied. There must be something—we could buy food in the morning, but for tonight? Under his pressure the staff found eggs, bread, butter in a can, tea. Trained to grateful acceptance as we were, it was a feast. We tarried in the kitchen with Joe and the staff; there were three of them, which is as many as only the rest houses of more important places have.

Two of them were men, one small and one taller and lean and impregnated with the aromatic smoke of the wood-burning stove. The third was a girl, as large as both the men in one, a female edifice, poker-faced, sparse of speech and slow in movement. She moved massively, letting her slow eyes rest upon one for heavy moments before words came, dropping singly. Was she, I wondered, studying her swelling forms, pregnant? I muttered to Kay.

'It's hard to tell, isn't it?' Kay muttered back.

It was not till next day, after overt study, that we knew she was pregnant and I could not suppress curiosity as to the achieving of that. When she stood near me her knees seemed to stand high against my height. She was not a very fat girl, just abundantly solid over the heavy bone.

It was pleasant in the stone-floored kitchen, becoming friendly in the smoke while the food was prepared. The small man bustled without haste, fetching wood to feed the belching stove and the taller one stood there, half seen, to do the cooking. The girl moved in and out, kitchen to dining-room, and at each passing the weight of her eyes under the lids slid over us sidelong. I saw soon that there was an expression working there. It never developed much but, I came to see, she was showing friendship.

When the food was ready she carried it to the dining-room and Joe, satisfied, took his leave.

'I will be back soon, when you have eaten. We will go to the club. We will have some beer. I will see you soon.'

And back he was soon, leading us out and into the Land Rover and through the tracks under the trees to come to the club. It was a low building, a bungalow like all the rest, put down almost, it seemed, where it happened to drop, and then the jacarandas and bougainvilleas and frangipani had gathered round it. The door stood open and the lights were just going on as we went in— candles here and there and a dim paraffin pressure lamp for the bar counter. The floor was concrete and there were round tables and chairs and a dart board. A man and a woman were behind the bar and company was beginning to gather for the evening.

Joe guided us to a table and then fetched beer, three bottles served in the standard fashion, with the crown tops lifted. You drink from the bottle. This we did, the three of us, but with the slight ceremony due to the occasion. Joe was still, so to speak, in his official chair; he raised his bottle, bidding us welcome to the community of Balovale, and we raised ours. Then we put back our heads, sucked at the bottles and gurgled in proper formal unison. That was pretty well the end of formality. We soon had more bottles and became very relaxed. Others joined us, there were innumerable introductions, voices rose and we all laughed a lot and it was happy. Only one thing differentiated us—I had a white sweating face in the twilight and everyone else had a black sweating face.

At first anyway. Then the young man from the English Midlands came in. He was doing his Voluntary Service there, three years in Balovale as Librarian. I think he was very pleased to have a little change of company, and perhaps he was particularly in need of new stimulation in feminine company. The impact upon him of Kay could be felt. It was he, I think, who suggested we should play darts and he elected himself to partner Kay. It did not really matter who partnered whom because there was little risk of anyone winning. It was a very informal game with no too great fussing about exactitude of the rules, and I was not sure how many of us were playing. My team seemed to vary from about four to six or seven and the opposition was no more defined. Nor did any one show such skill as to embarrass the ineptitude of the rest of us. With the inevitability of such games of darts we came in time to stalemate, both sides needing double-one to win. There, vaguely and at no specific time, the game ended. But it had been a very happy game and we all drank to that.

Joe took us shopping in the morning and that could have been regarded as a revelation of what is happening in the distant heart of Africa. Anywhere in Zambia you are a thousand miles from the sea, and Balovale (or Zambezi as it now is) is a long way from

Zambia's capital, Lusaka. It is a remote provincial centre, so recently nearly inaccessible. And now, there in the broad central street, against the inky latticed shade of the jacarandas, was the modern store. It was, African fashion, all on one floor and, Balovale fashion, carelessly lavish with space. It was huge inside, vistaed with shelves and counters. I think it could not long have been newly opened; everything sparkled with fresh newness and the stacked goods were barely broached. They had not finished with the floor; a surface was still being applied to it, some sort of polish finish being painted on and buffed up. It shone, and we, exploring among the shelves, first slipped and slid clutching at the air and then went slowly on shuffled feet.

The shelves bore everything, a canned cornucopia, all fruits, all meats, cereals, sugars, spices, preserves, every kind of food that can come processed, canned, or in any way ingeniously packaged. It was so strange, hardly real, to us who had just stepped out of the hungry bush and the sheer quantity seemed devised for emphasis. I suppose it was a clear demonstration of progress, of Africa striding into the great modern world. But for all that is was worrying.

Africa has had, traditionally, feeding problems, and has them now. Famine has been and is too familiar. Malnutrition stalks the villages. There has been much death from those causes and from the old indigenous diseases and, however harsh the logic of it, that has been within the frame of nature which demands that the populations of the various species shall remain within the feeding capacity of the environment. Many who were born did not survive, but those who did were tough and untouched by the degenerative diseases that menace the life of every citizen of a modern western country. Those western diseases have been totally unknown in primitive societies such as those of Africa. Modern western man invented the diseases and assiduously promoted them with his modern processed foods and soft living.

But what humane person, what government, could see the

want in Africa, the hungry children, skinny-framed and big-bellied and not seek to do anything that can by any means be done? A child sickening out of life from malnutrition or sheer hunger is something not to be argued about. Nothing matters, it seems, but succour. Ready and reliable access to food ample enough to cancel all the old distresses must be provided. So, surely, it is splendid, heartening and entirely admirable to see the fine new stores coming to all the Balovales of Africa.

Yes—to bring food, to cancel the unbearable sight of hungry children—that *is* something to clutch at. But—should we exchange for that distressing thing something which must in the end be a greater evil?

Nature has operated a pitiless principle to balance population and environment. All compassion demands that we should qualify it, and that means, to be truly practical, that we improve the environment's yield of good food so as to alter the equation. That will work, will have the effect sought, if the population does not also increase as the yield of food increases—and that is an inherent danger in any increase in availability of food.

I will not pretend that all this filled my mind that morning at Balovale. To all those ranks of food we reacted as hungry people from the villages have done. We stocked up. We went laden with Joe to the Land Rover. He stayed with us in the kitchen smoke to watch the cooking of lunch.

'Enjoy your lunch,' he said. 'I will come afterwards for you. We will go to the river. It will be hot and we will swim. It will be nice.'

It was. He came about two, beaming and round, and on the way to the river the Land Rover filled up. We stopped here and there where people waited and others came running and waving and climbing aboard until the vehicle bulged with the laughing sweating cram. We were extruded just above the river and there were others already there on the white sweep of sand. Some were swimming and I supposed that the place was known to be normally free of crocodiles though, as I knew, they were common enough just upstream. Probably there, against the town, they had been shot down assiduously.

Nobody was worrying about crocodiles, or about anything else. There was the sun, high and hot, the sand was soft and the river was cool. The present was perfect; it was a delight like the year-long summer afternoons of childhood to lie in the roasting sand making idly profound conversation till it dwindled, then roll over and into the water. Joe and I, face downward with cheeks in the sand, got to the bottom of several very significant matters of which I remember no fragment, then slid into the river where the rest of the uproarious throng swam and splashed like dogs. The young man from the Midlands had come and was attentive to Kay.

'Bring your rod,' Joe had said, and now I climbed dripping into a boat that someone had brought and sat in my own puddle as we sped across the river to try for a tiger. We caught a few, sudden eruptions from the water, wrenching and hurtling for a time before ferocious yielding. Then back to the sand and the water and the gregarious idling until the afternoon began to shorten and it was time to brush off the caked sand and dress and drift from the beach.

The white man came just then. I did not see where he came from; he was there, walking slowly in white shirt and white shorts, carrying a gun, passing through the jostling crowd without seeming to see them. He seemed to be alone in an empty place, with his mournful eyes passing through and beyond those in his path. He did see me. He stopped. His voice was English.

'I've been here a long time,' he said when he had looked dully into my eyes for a time. 'Yes, a long time. I often come here in the evening. Looking for something to shoot. I usually try to find something to shoot.'

He gazed sadly at me for a little longer and then seemed to lose me. I saw him last as a vaguely wandering figure in the distance.

At the club that night it was as it had been the night before, with the darts game as inconsequentially threading the hours and the young man from the Midlands as modestly and unobtrusively devoting himself to Kay. I believe she really was unaware. Balovale being a town—however airily spacy and flowery a town— it kept later hours than the villages, the difference between town and country being in Africa much as it is elsewhere. It was fully ten o'clock, so late, when we left the club, and still with our evening not ended. We went with Joe. His wife was away, he said, but if we would forgive that he would be so happy if we would come to his home for a drink. How we came to Joe's house, where it was, I had no idea. In the Land Rover we doubled through the twined labyrinth under the trees and through the blossoms till such navigational sense as the evening had left me had been made a cat's cradle. We stopped and there was Joe's house, nearly lost in the scrambling embrace of bougainvillea. The clinging air was warm, heavy with the scent of frangipani.

Joe was shy now, ushering us over the verandah and into his house, modestly self-conscious at taking us into his privacy. It was cosy in a western fashion, with a pretty frill of curtaining and many books on the shelves. Conversation, I think, must have turned on books though I am vague about it; but something did prompt me to the round declaration that there is as richly fine writing in the Old Testament as can be found between covers and to hell with all meddlers who 'modernize' and utterly debilitate the gorgeous text. What, I remember hearing myself ask rhetorically, is there to better or even equal the *Song Of Solomon*, that glorious roll of words? I asked that and at once there was Joe's big bible on my lap and he fingering it through to find the *Song*.

'You will read it?' he asked, and I did, and how well or badly

I cannot know; but, I believe, with ample feeling. I hope the others were past their keenest judgement. The young man from the Midlands was not listening anyway; his whole attention was on Kay. The rest of the evening was mellow if, seen from this distance, a little inchoate. I think it was prolonged from an irking sense of farewell—in the morning we must leave Balovale. It had been a happy place.

We must get to Lukulu downstream; there were problems in that. Between Balovale and Lukulu tributary rivers came in, and we could see no means for the crossing of them, especially the Kabompo River, a major tributary. Advance worrying at that had suggested that we should be air lifted out of Balovale and put down at Lukulu and from there make such way as we could upstream and downstream. Study of the map suggested that that was something to be approached with a crossing of the fingers; I had heard that it was remotely isolated country.

Joe came with us in the morning to the airstrip. I was not surprised to see the young man from the Midlands waiting when we came. We had to wait for the aeroplane for the best part of an hour and as we talked away the time, Joe, Kay, and I, the young man mostly stood modestly by looking at Kay. When it did come, when we had squeezed in, about to take off, the last of Balovale that I saw was the round and friendly Joe, waving vigorously and the young man standing with a limp lift of one arm. He looked dumbly sad. I was sorry for him.

9

Lukulu was fascinating in anticipation. There, for the first time, we would have left the adolescent upper reaches of the river, out of North Western Province, into Western Province. Western Province used to be Barotse Province and before that Barotseland. It is saturated with the tradition and lore of the Barotse people and particularly the great Lozi tribe. Kay is Lozi, royal Lozi, a relative of the Litunga, a thing demonstrated by the ivory bracelets she wears. The Litungas were formerly kings of Barotseland and now are paramount chiefs of special eminence. Lukulu is the gateway to the Barotse country as you come from the north.

It stands on a great bend of the river on the last of the high ground scarped up from the river, just ahead of the great Barotse flood plain. There the ground lies low and, every rainy season, the water comes out of the banks and fills the plain to the horizon.

It is also Livingstone country; his imprint is indelible, and the more so because it was near Lukulu, a few miles upstream, that he made one of his rare geographical mistakes. I had the feeling that if I could go there, to that same place, see that which he had misconstrued, I should have a keener sense of the man. I could perhaps conjure the sense of his coming there with his first discoverer's eye, even in imagination see as he saw. It was in that part of the river between Balovale and Lukulu which I had had to jump that he, going upstream, had come to a confluence. Two rivers joined, one coming in from the east and one coming down from the north. One was the main Zambezi and one was a tribu-

Stalking a meal

At the Jimbe River

tary. He has left his hand-drawn map as evidence and Balovale he has lettered in as *Balobale*. The main river he calls *Leeambye* or *Zambezi*—it was also spelt *Liambye*—and at the confluence he shows the river out of the east as the 'R. Leeambye or main stream of Zambezi'. The other, the stream from the north, he writes in as the R. Leeba, a tributary which he shows as becoming small and lost. But the course he shows for it *is* pretty accurately that of the main Zambezi which I had followed from the source. His 'R. Leeambye or main stream of Zambezi' is the Kabompo River, a tributary, though a considerable one. He, it is said, saw the Kabompo as the bigger stream and so concluded that it was the main stream. I felt a compulsion to go there to see if I too saw it so. My map showed no justification for that—it showed the main river unmistakably bigger than the Kabompo.

So then, if, at Lukulu, I could get those facilities which I had failed to get so far but which had been essential to my original plan—if I could get stores, camping gear and bearers—I could explore with the freedom needed, with no dependence upon a fixed base. I could go upstream to the Kabompo confluence as Livingstone had done. That had been an additional reason for the air hop—to come as Livingstone had come. That achieved, I could go with the river downstream from Lukulu, through the huge void of the plain till I came to Mongu. Mongu is the capital place of the Barotse country, tribal centre of the Lozi. It is also Kay's birthplace and we had begun to have a sense of pilgrimage about that.

We touched down about mid-morning, rolling to a stop on the blank white blaze of the airstrip. We had buzzed the place first as the custom is, making several low sweeps over it to alert whoever should be expecting us and now we looked out expectantly. There would, we hoped, be a Land Rover to pick us up, to be a sign that all was in hand. We saw nothing.

We climbed out. There seemed to be nothing, nothing but the

empty scorch of the airstrip, no sound, no person, no building. Then we saw at the strip's end, distant in the air's quiver, a low hut. Two figures stood in its shade. We walked towards it.

The two men at the hut were white, squinting through the dazzle, one bearded, smiling in vaguely friendly fashion as if he did not want us to make too much of it, the other tall, blond, large-boned and lean. Both were in white shirts and shorts, absently flicking the flies away as they waited non-committally for us to make an opening.

I told them I thought we were expected. Did they by any chance know anything of that—or had they come to meet us? They shook their heads slowly. I explained that I understood that the District Secretary had been informed and would be providing help. No, they knew nothing of that—they were from the Mission. The bearded one had begun to edge back, gently backing away from the possibility of involvement. His aspect of kindly goodness became more bland as he murmured something about his need to get back to the Mission.

The tall one had been regarding us thoughtfully. Then he spoke, suddenly purposefully.

'You will come with me. You will come to my house. You will stay in my house and have food—and you will pay me. *Ja?* Come, my Land Rover is over there. We will load your gear from the aeroplane. That will be good, *ja?*'

He smiled, showing very large white teeth while his light blue eyes looked cool and measuring. He led us towards the aircraft walking with a long loping stride, then handling the gear with curt efficiency. We passed abruptly from the naked blaze of the airstrip into Lukulu, going suddenly from its wilderness into the arcaded walks under the trees. Like Balovale, the whole place lay under the open colonnading of the trees, jacaranda, flamboyant, the various acacias, the vistas wreathed with bougainvillea, ipomaea, and frangipani. It was small though, unlike Balovale,

small and beautiful, the more so that all its low buildings were
white. Mainly they were mission buildings. There was little of
Lukulu that was not mission. Beyond, straggling away from the
priestly nucleus, were the huts and garden plots of the people.

We came to the house of our host (whom I will call Hellmuth)
and he pushed the Land Rover into the shade of a mango tree,
forcing under so that the unripe fruits drummed on roof and
sides.

'This is my house,' he said. 'Come in—you will stay here, *ja*?
Now we will have some food.' He led us into the kitchen and
beyond into a sitting-room. The first impression was that it was
aerially poised above the river. The small enclosure of garden,
planted with groundnuts—rather like low-growing peas—was
below the window and went to the edge of the abrupt drop to
the river. The view, not quite on the very point of the great bend,
was downstream. Beyond the gardens lay the river, receding
enormously into level distance. It was huge now, a pale blue plane
of water. From Lukulu the ground fell steeply to it, a tangle of
bananas, sisal plots, maize gardens, straggling verticals of pawpaw,
spiky silhouettes of oil palms. That was the last of high ground.
For all the way with the river into remote distance the land was
as low and level as the water. There under our eminence was the
Barotse flood plain.

We sat at the kitchen table when the servant brought food and
Hellmuth crossed himself. We waited while he murmured with
dropped head. While we ate he worked in a staccato fashion to
make conversation, telling us that he was there for a period with
the mission to inculcate more modern techniques of agriculture.
He lived in the mission's house and worked with the people of
Lukulu and the villages nearby. What did we want to do immediately? What were our plans? When I told him he said he would
take us that afternoon to the Boma.

The Boma lay away from the mission's central place under the trees, along a mile or more of sun-parched dirt road through scrub. At the Boma the air was dizzy with heat; those there looked at us with deep absence of interest. No, they said, the District Secretary was not there that day—perhaps he would be tomorrow or another day. It seemed to be of enormous indifference when he would be there. Was there anyone there who could help, we asked; could anyone say if we were likely to be able to get bearers and stores? It appeared that nothing could be less likely.

I had explained to Hellmuth that I must get up-river to the Kabompo confluence and, that done, make my way down-river to Mongu. If I could not get bearers, if I were not able to go on foot to the Kabompo, what then asked Hellmuth? Would I go by boat if one could be found? That recalled something half forgotten, perhaps not even true, that Livingstone had gone partly by boat and partly by bank—had he not gone by boat with another party making way on the shore? I could not remember but it was enough. Yes, I said, if a boat could be found that is the way I would go. There is a boat at the Mission, Hellmuth declared. We might be able to have use of it. He thought the Irish fathers had it.

We found a priest at the Mission, a pallid fair man. He regarded Kay and me askance. We did not make a favourable impression. He stood with feet apart; I noticed how closely he filled his shirt and pale blue shorts. His full-bottomed face was lowered, he looked at us coldly. No, he could not help. The Irish fathers might. They had a boat.

The Irish fathers were in a bungalow at the most sublime point of panorama above the river. One of them opened the door a little way at our knocking. He listened, looking at the ground while Hellmuth explained. Then he came out on to the verandah, pulling the door to behind him and now suddenly he smiled with a twinkle of blue eyes. Ah sure yes, he would like to help us, he would like us to be able to get to the Kabompo confluence in their boat. But he thought the boat was out of order—what a pity. And goodbye to us and good luck. Then the door shut. The weight of Lukulu's indifference to us was becoming oppressive. I began to feel an urge to move on, get out. Suppose we cannot get bearers; would it be possible for a boat to come up from Mongu? Was there a way of communicating with Mongu, with the D.S. there? 'We will go back to the Boma,' said Hellmuth. 'The police have radio—perhaps they will let you talk to Mongu, *ja?*'

The Boma still crouched nakedly in the swim of heat—for some reason it seemed more aridly scorched there than elsewhere, more enervatingly frying—but the police were amiable and ready to be helpful even if, at first, preserving the official mask. Yes, they would try to put us on to the D.S. at Mongu—but, we must understand, there was police business too and we must wait until there should be a space in radio time.

We waited. The slow hot afternoon went on weighted minutes; flies swarmed and pestered, cicadas sang dizzily, lizards paused and darted and looked with little gleams of jewelled eyes. An enormous *ennui* sat on the place—or perhaps it sat just on us. The feeling had begun to grow that we were caught in a trap of timelessness and non-event from which there was no exit. I walked along the front of the Boma, back and forth, then tired of that and went round the side of it and along the back. I stood under the only tree in the sun-scorched vacancy and looked at the myriad insects all living out separate existences in the furrows of bark. That made me feel more lost in some sort of limbo. There were so many creatures here, from bugs to priests, absorbed in their own ways, unwilling to stir out of them enough to take cognizance of us.

But shape, and some hope, returned when the police called. They were in contact with the Boma at Mongu. Kay went to speak. She spoke to the D.S., she explained who we were and what we were about, and what our predicament was. Since it was virtually certain, in the absence of the D.S. at Lukulu, that we should get no bearers, could a boat come up from Mongu so that we could go up to the Kabompo confluence, then make our way down-river to Mongu? The answer was indeterminate but with ample willingness to be helpful. Almost certainly there could be a boat. Perhaps tomorrow. Would we communicate again tomorrow? We left the Boma a little cheered.

The evening was long. Night fell, and the hours stretched ahead. About seven the servant brought food, and after Hellmuth had crossed himself and murmured, we ate it. Then we sat in the sitting-room.

'Well,' said Hellmuth, 'now we talk, *ja*? Now we have conversation.' He smiled and looked briskly anticipating, leaning back a little with a straight back. He waited expectantly, looking at me. I groped, striving to seize and pin down a topic. My mind was as empty as an inverted bucket. I looked at Kay. She was looking straight ahead; she said nothing. Across the room, on the sofa, there was Hellmuth, still erectly leaning back, with crossed legs, smiling and waiting for me. The ordering of his day had come to evening—it was the time for relaxation.

Conversation never did get off the ground. It made staccato starts, like a faulty engine, starting and stuttering for short whiles, then dying. We went to bed about nine. Kay had a room; I lay on the sitting-room floor and found it hard. I had my sleeping bag, but it was too hot to sleep inside it. I lay on top of it; the hardness of the floor seemed to dissolve its substance. It was while I was still wanly trying to accommodate my hip to the unyielding floor that I woke. The sun was climbing and it was after five.

We were early at the Boma to get a place in the queue for radio time. The police were friendly now—we were the old friends of yesterday—and yes, they would try to get us on to Mongu as soon as they could. We waited and when we had waited only a little while the D.S. appeared. He came out of his office and stood on the verandah. He stood about five feet and had an imperious stance. His head was slightly back so that his huge black beard had an outthrust. Under his white shirt and dark blue shorts he was inclined to paunchiness. I thought that his chubby legs had a very confident look.

'There is the D.S.,' somebody said, and Kay approached him. He did not look at her until she was right up to him and then he looked at her coldly from under his lids. That was awkward because she was taller than he. Kay explained; he listened and with tilted head rested haughty eyes on the horizon. A telegram had been sent to him, Kay added, informing him in advance of what she had told him.

'Might get here in about a fortnight,' he said distantly, then turned to speak to Kay. His haughty backthrown gaze was directed over her shoulder.

'I have heard your remarks,' he said, and he was very severe and cold. 'I have noted your requests. I have to tell you that it is of no interest to me. I have my official duties to take my attention. That is all.' He turned and walked away.

Boat or nothing then. We must wait and wait we did through all the leaden moments of the morning. I wandered in aimless suspension about the Boma, looking at this and looking at that and not really seeing anything. Not until I saw the beetle. That arrested me. It was a magnificent creature.

It was splendid and enamelled and shining, three inches or more long with wing cases heart-shaped, three-quarters of an inch across, and brilliant mahogany. Its thorax was engraved with deep ridges, its formidable jaws crossed like scissors. I called to Kay, telling her of it, and when it heard my voice a shiver ran through it. It began to walk, looking like a beautifully fantastic mechanical thing; as it went I went with it, setting up my camera.

'I must have its portrait,' I told Kay, and she and all the Boma messengers stood by watching. I went bent, as if on all fours, peering through the camera, with a splayed foot and straddled leg either side. The more closely I attended the more disturbed it became, the more it scuttled, turning and doubling erratically. I went with it, crab-like, crouched and scuttling too. The Boma messengers came behind, following but so nearly helpless with laughter that it was difficult. They reeled, wept with laughter. My photographs, when developed, were not good. They were blurred.

Blank somnolence descended again, the hot minutes dragging, the sense growing of having been cancelled. I walked inconsequentially, here and there, trying to keep some feeling of action. One of the Boma messengers came to me.

'Where do you come from, Bwana? Why do you come here?'

'I come from England. I have come here to write a book, a book about the river.'

'When you have finished here will you go back to England?'

'Yes, I shall go back.'

'Then, Bwana, when you go back to England, will you take me with you so that I can become a book writer?'

'Why—do you want to be a book writer?'

'Ah, yes, Bwana, I do. I do want to be a book writer. That is my ambition.'

He looked at me with earnest intensity. I have often wondered since about him; I recall his eyes. I see their pleading. Had he an unexpressed vocation or was it romanticism? If he had a true capacity, Lukulu was a remotely inappropriate place for it. The thought of him comes to worry me at times.

Towards the end of the morning the police summoned us; they had Mongu for us. Would Kay talk to the D.S. again? The D.S. was reassuring. There would be a boat, he said, he would send it up-river for us. Kay asked when it would come. He might be able to send it today—it could be at Lukulu by evening. We dare not give that too much belief; but I knew that later that day we should be straining our ears. The sound of an engine on the river carries a long way.

'You will come with me this afternoon, *ja?*' asked Hellmuth over lunch. Yes, I said, I would go with him though I did not know where he was going. To go anywhere was action. We went to a village a few miles from Lukulu.

Hellmuth loaded the Land Rover with sacks of mealie meal, immense sacks which he handled and swung aboard with abrupt and dominating ease. We went out of Lukulu on a track a foot deep in white dust, running downstream and parallel with the river for about two miles and then swinging away into the bush. It was open bush, with high blanched grass and scrub and flat-topped thorn trees making inky patches of shade. The Land Rover lurched and skidded through the serpentine track; when I was sure that it went to nowhere we came to a village. It was very small, half a dozen huts, a scattering of children, a few women and a leper. He went upon a crutch, but because his thin arms terminated in shrivelled lumps, his wrist was lashed to the crutch. His legs were wasted and he had not feet but knobs, enlarging a little from the ankles. One was roughly wrapped to shield it from the ground. He was a cheerful man, laughing and twinkling, hobbling agilely and crackling with what I think were little jokes.

Another man appeared from behind a hut, eager, rather ingratiating and chirping. It was for him that Hellmuth had brought the mealie meal. We should bring it into his hut he said, and went as if to handle it in himself. But the sacks were as high as he and vastly bulkier. He struggled, striving to throw his short arms round a sack. As it shifted and leaned and was manifestly going to crush him to the ground, Hellmuth put his arms to it without apparent flexion of muscle and carried it into the hut. He carried in the others, two more, and we followed him into the hut. The light was dim, filtering through the interlaced grasses of walls and roof; there were two compartments divided by a grass partition.

A girl came from behind the partition, showing herself timidly and then backing uncertainly against the wall. She was about sixteen, pretty, and advancedly pregnant.

The man giggled, with his eyebrows jerking upwards apprehensively. 'This is my sister,' he said.

Hellmuth looked at her with his long fair face blank and his blue eyes like glass marbles. Then he turned slowly to the man.

'She is married, *ja?*' He still smiled slightly, but his voice rose at his sentence's end with a hard note of interrogation.

'Yes, yes, yes, she is married.' The little man laughed, stood on his toes and made reassuring passes with his hands.

'That is good.' The matter of the girl was dealt with. Hellmuth turned with unemotional briskness to other things. The girl stood with her hands behind her, picking nervously at the fibres of grass in the wall. Perhaps she even is married I thought.

When we left the village the children shrieked farewell, the women waved, the little man waved with a relief he could not hide (though I do not think Hellmuth saw it), and the leper hobbled agitatedly, trying to run after us.

We stood a long time at the edge above the river that evening, straining our eyes and listening. There was no sound, no sight of a boat but the dug-out canoes of men fishing. We sat out the long blank evening with Hellmuth and anticipated another morning at the Boma. We were there soon after seven.

Again we waited through the endless accumulation of minutes and now we were not the only ones who waited. The implementation of justice hung upon what the radio should bring. A man sat staring before him, swaying sickly. His head was heavily swathed with bandages. The day before, they told us, he had been hit on the head with a bottle; it had broken his skull. Now he waited, sitting on the edge of the verandah. Not far from him sat another man who also waited. He was the assailant; he waited to be charged.

'All right. Bring him in,' the police had said when the injured man had come with his complaint. He, hardly able to totter, had gathered his relatives. They and he brought in the assailant; now all waited by the Boma, squatting in the dust and sitting on the verandah till decision should come on the radio. Our call came towards midday, and, yes, the D.S. at Mongu said, it is arranged. The boat is setting off. It will be at Lukulu by nightfall.

We did not believe or disbelieve. We were doing what we could and what would come would come; most probably nothing would come. In the afternoon I went with Hellmuth to where the people had their plantations.

'I must show them what to do. You can walk, *ja*? You can go walking a long way down the river and I find you later, *ja*?'

We went two miles or so down-river from the mission centre, to where the gardens dropped down to the river's swampy margin and, above, the huts clustered among the bananas and mangoes and pawpaws. At a maize plot a man and his wife were working, moving slowly, stirring the soil between the plants.

'Come. I show them,' Hellmuth said. He got out of the Land Rover, snatched from it a big bag of artificial fertilizer and went down the drop from the track to the maize plot with ostrich strides. There he gathered up the man and his wife as a bustling wind gathers up leaves. He swept them to the upper end of the plot then, as they stood submissively, he explained the fine modern medicine of artificial fertilizers. Your plants will grow like giants and they will fill many big baskets with grain, was the effect of what he told them. They listened with total unemotion, limply respectful. He filled lesser bags for them, showed them how to toss to the root of each plant a handful and then commanded them each to a row while he started on another. They went slowly, bending to each plant, taking a handful, putting it to the root. He burned down the row, going like something mechanical that dazes with its incredible ingenuity, dipping, lifting, scooping, shooting, every movement precise and quick and regular. They were halfway on a first row when he swept by, doubling back on his second row.

He stopped for a moment at the end of the row.

'You can walk now, *ja*? You want to walk down the Zambezi —you walk now. I will see you later.' Then he had started again, dip, lift, dip, lift.

I watched for a few minutes and then began to walk, threading a way through the plots of maize and sisal and groundnuts, thinking mournfully that while the developed countries of the West are considering what can be done to restore to their soils the fertility destroyed by chemical fertilizers, African countries are being hustled into destroying theirs by the same certain means without the intervening centuries of good husbandry and fertility that the West has enjoyed. Traditionally Africans have worked their land for subsistence farming, working a village plot or burning off a piece of bush, and growing what will feed the family.

'Now we are teaching them cash farming,' I had been told at one of the missions, and very ominous I had thought that. The old way of burning a patch, planting it for a year and then moving on to burn another, may seem a wanton way with land and only poorly productive. So it is of course and its weakness has shown tragically in many famine years. Rotational and organic farming, returning to the soil what is taken from it, could bring poignantly needed benefit.

I went on, skirting the plots lying down the slope in the drenching sunlight. They were dug anywhere where the land had rooting depth over the rock and was dry enough between the quaking marshes. They were precariously gained from the wild; the high reedy grasses, oil palms and shrubby thickets would obviously take them back in a few weeks of neglect. It was beautiful there, poised above the river's enormous vista hanging in the heat haze. I went slowly.

There was an arum growing against the track, fleshily beautiful, organic seeming and more than merely plant. Its succulent outer leaves enclosed the deep plum-coloured, plastic-smooth erectile centre. As I admired it I saw what I took to be a brilliant tiny bird. It took flight, the size of a wren, with a wren's flight, vividly mauve. I followed its flight till it pitched fifty yards away. I walked on, and another took flight. Now there were many of them, some mauve, some straw-coloured, bursting from the plants, going forty or fifty yards and settling—but not, as I soon saw, birds; a sort of grasshopper. So I thought, and then realized they were locusts. I had not seen locusts before; I had not been prepared for the beauty of them. The stories of locusts, the half-horror of them, suggests something loathsome, something creepingly pestilential. Here were these creatures, startlingly beautiful, flying in the sunlight, looking as harmless and delightful as butterflies. So they are until they multiply, fly in myriad hordes that denude whole countrysides. At other times in other places they may be present as ordinarily as grasshoppers, hardly more damaging.

Walk, Hellmuth had said; here is your chance he had implied, make the most of it, and walk I did, aimlessly. Mongu lay down the river, beyond the level horizon, a long long walk away, not the stuff of an afternoon's perambulation. So I pottered; I pottered down through the garden plots to the marginal swamp and oozy wilderness by the water, stumbled too far and dragged myself out to walk on squelching. I pottered beyond the plots and met the children and the women returning to the huts under the palms and bananas; I talked to the rolling dusty-bellied piccaninns outside the huts, trying to win smiles. Mostly they stood, arrested in their affairs in the dust, with open mouths and guarded incomprehension. For the whole afternoon I wandered and idled where the gardens grew and the people lived and everything was pleasant and easy away from the pressure of the mission. I would walk back into Lukulu, I decided finally, not wait to be picked up by

Hellmuth, and, as I plodded the deep dust of the track above the plots, back towards Lukulu, I saw Hellmuth. He was still busy in the maize, far ahead of the man and his wife, working through the rows like a wonderful mechanical thing.

We listened by the river in the evening. We heard the far carry of voices of men in their canoes half a mile and more away on the river. We heard the fish eagle and the kites and watched the perpetually wheeling vultures beyond the river. All the sounds and sights of any evening; but nothing else. No sound of an engine, no sight of a boat tiny and distant down the river. We had not really expected the boat would come.

We went only perfunctorily to the Boma next morning to be told the boat was coming. I left without demur when Hellmuth asked me if I would go to the market with him. Like the gardens, it was away from the mission, out of the claustrophobia, among the people. Its focus was a store, the usual long-fronted verandahed building where you can buy brilliant fabrics from the stacked bales, or canned foods, or crates of beer. The market was hitched to the store, the whole space filled with people selling cassava, rank on rank of sacks each with its squatting attendant, man or woman; so much cassava and so many people selling cassava. I wondered who there could be to buy cassava. I saw no one. There *was* a ceaseless noisy business there, but nothing but the perpetual high-pitched banter and laughter that there always is when the people are together and at ease in the sun. There was not the least point of difference between one man's cassava and the next except that a few had it as meal though most had it as short-lengthed root. Cassava, mainstay of every meal, is a root, fat and round, belonging to a low-growing shrub. It peels white, looking waxily succulent, and in every village you will see the women pounding it to fine white meal in wooden mortars.

The rest of the market was across the road, in caves of shade under the mangoes, people and flies, children and dogs all in a noisy leisurely milling among the flimsy stalls. Several of the stalls had for sale minute quantities of groundnuts. Some of the stalls had tobacco, rolls of what seemed to be the untreated natural leaf whipped up. I bought some after a brief show of bargaining and, at the seller's insistence, tried it. It was a sensation rather than a taste, hot, without flavour. I did not try the fish, nor stay near the stalls long. It was sun-dried and practically intolerably high smelling—fish of all sizes, shrivelled whitebait-size up to quite large tilapia. Tilapia is a universal African food fish, for good reason. It thrives in all sort of waters, rivers and lakes, multiplies freely and is hardy in terms of a tropical environment.

I did try the drink, both sorts. It was sold by women who sat, with their children, in the dust by the road. I had the *sipechu* first, in a big enamel mug. I did not care for it. It was newly made, brought straight and very recently from the brewing. It was warm, nearly hot, and looked like dirty milk. *Sipechu* is maize beer, very highly regarded, not at all ill-tasting if not irresistible.

The other drink was *kachipembe*, and I tried that too. I had expected it to be in some way compulsive, but I expect you have to persevere. To be so notorious I thought, it must be seductive. But in the remote villages the range of rot-gut is limited—there is bottled beer at the stores; after that you must make it yourself. My *kachipembe*, like the *sipechu*, was warm and like very thin and murky skimmed milk. I did quite like the taste.

The boat did not come that evening. We listened for it because to stand above the lucent sweep of the river in the changing light was better than to fret elsewhere. The enormous impersonal peace of the evening was mournfully sweet.

We walked upstream in the morning, as if going to the Kabompo confluence, though we knew we should not get there. The round trip, there and back to Lukulu, was close to fifty miles —two days' walking in the best conditions. Now the early coming of the rains had increased humidity and our trudging, skirting the swamps and diverging for the thorn thickets, brought us to limp saturation in an hour. But we had to walk out of Lukulu to lessen our sense of being trapped there. I think our walking increased the sense of our trappedness. The more naked miles of sun-bitten bush we walked the more inevitably we knew we must walk them back into the clutch of Lukulu. We watched men poling upstream in dug-out canoes laden to the gunwales with cassava sacks, and knew they were going to their villages. We saw an elderly man naked in a canoe under the bank; he was washing in river water, lathering himself and falling into an agony of modesty when we came by. He belonged to a cluster of huts half a mile away into the bush; he and all the life of the place were going their ordinary way. We were of no consequence to it. We walked on till it became futile, then sat in the inadequate checkering of shade of a thorn tree. We stared at the hot blue sky and it seemed hostile.

Thirst moved us. We had seen a village a mile or two distant inland from the river; if it had a store there would be beer. There was, and we sat on the verandah's edge to drink it. In the way of village stores a man on the verandah sat at a very old treadle sewing machine running up for the women the flaring lengths of material bought from the bales inside. Outside the people sat with their beer under the trees, in the grass-roofed shelter there. It was pleasant; then the D.S. arrived in his Land Rover. He strutted by, contriving, with back-thrown head and haughty droop of lids, not to see us.

It was only a mile or so to walk from there to Lukulu, but every foot was multiplied. A road it would be called, constantly used, a broad sun-drowned way, white hot. The coming and going on it was constant, a slow drift of knots and clusters of people gaudily bright with printed cottons. It was hard to walk—the surface— so loosely soft and deep with dust that every step was as nearly backward as forward. Humidity made the going worse—the air which

Boys bathing at Chavuma

Women with fish baskets, Balovale

had been dry and firm had become a sponge. The least movement brought a gout of sweat; energy was sapped.

Kay was wearing a man's shirt, a man's jeans, a man's socks. We passed a group of women, all in their brilliant cottons swagged and tucked, with flaring head scarves. One who was large and ageing, putting her weight with care from foot to foot, looked at Kay, and spoke carefully to those with her. Her face was not expressive but I discerned perplexity.

'What did she say?' I asked Kay.

'She said, "Now that is strange. I do not understand that. This man walks like a woman, is the size of a woman, has the shape of a woman. I do not understand that." '

We came gratefully into Lukulu. There was shade in Lukulu. The mango trees were dense-crowned, there were many of them; their thick and polished leaves are wonderful excluders of the sun.

Hellmuth was in the house. 'The boat does not come, *ja*?' He looked from one to the other of us. 'But you do not want to stay in Lukulu?'

We said we did not.

'You will come with me then, tomorrow? I go in the Land Rover to Mongu. I take you and you pay me. You pay me for staying in my house and when we get to Mongu you pay me for taking you there in the Land Rover?'

It would be farewell; I did not expect to come back to Lukulu. But I did, a year later. I suppose now is the time to tell of that, because it was the Kabompo confluence which brought me back.

My business at Lukulu had not been done. I had been so near the Kabompo confluence, so near; but I did not see it. Go I must, by land or by river. So, after a year, I came back, flying in again, for no other purpose than to get to the Kabompo confluence. This becomes the story of how, after all, I did not get there, by land or by water. But I did see it.

There had been preparation this time. Someone went in advance of my going to make sure all was well. He had talked to all concerned, collected assurances that there would be accommodation, a good powered boat, everything, absolutely everything necessary. I was confident when we climbed out of the aircraft on that same white and blinding airstrip. We had buzzed the place too.

There was nobody about. We waited, kicking the stones. Then yes, there was a Land Rover—but it seemed to be passing the end of the airstrip. It slowed, hesitated, then turned back and on to the airstrip. The tall man who got out told us that he was the District Governor—he was passing, saw us land. Could he help? Were we looking for anyone?

Why yes, we said, we were looking for him among others. We had a letter for him that explained all; and indeed he could help. We were relying on that.

'Ah yes, I see,' he said and read the letter. 'Now I'll just go off to arrange something, then I will come back.' He smiled encouragingly, got into the Land Rover and went. We waited, kicking the stones again.

We waited quite a long time, or it seemed so, half an hour perhaps. Then there was a Land Rover again. But not the D.G.'s— a smallish thin man got out, and he was anxious. He asked worriedly what we were there for. Could he help? We told him, and we told him about the D.G. He became more anxious—he was the Assistant District Secretary. When we said that it had been arranged that we should have a boat to go up to the Kabompo confluence, I began to feel sorry for him.

He wrung his hands. 'The D.G. will not be coming back. I have seen him. He was going to go off—in the boat—he was going to go bird shooting down the river.'

Now we shared his anxiety. But the boat we said, the boat—it had been firmly arranged that it was to be available. Could he hurry to the D.G. and tell him? He did, scurrying away, and was quite quickly back. The D.G. would take no notice and—he fluttered as he told us—the D.G. had gone. He had taken the boat and gone bird shooting down the river.

What *could* it be about Lukulu? How *could* it have such continuity of frustration that the year between was cancelled? Could we be sure to have the boat tomorrow then? Would the D.G. have finished his bird shooting? Perhaps, perhaps, yes certainly that would be so, and I could see that the A.D.S. in his deep unhappiness hoped very sincerely that that would be so. He recovered a little when we said all right, we would wait till tomorrow. He declined again immediately when we said that we knew that accommodation had been arranged and how obliged we would be if he would take us to it.

'Oh—has it? Oh yes, of course—well—we will go to the mission.' And, when we reached it, there it still was, just the same, the same cold depression as freshly remembered as if it had been a day not a year. The door was not opened very widely and it was only after the A.D.S. had talked for some time with anxious urgency that it opened enough for us to see the brother. He looked at the floor as we went in and said nothing. He took us across a courtyard, through a corridor, into a room hung with pious insignia of one sort and another. He did not look at us or speak to us, though there was Dave, who was pilot, another man, and myself. He suggested successfully that only he and the A.D.S. were present. He did not look at the A.D.S. either, but talked to him for a moment in a subdued monotone, then left us.

Silence hung in the room like a vapour. I felt as if I were being watched—and, I thought, the watcher does not feel like a friend. Not one of us spoke. I found myself hoping with fervour that we should not be given hospitality. When the brother, with drab blond face low-hung, came back he said nothing to us. Looking at the floor he spoke to the A.D.S. briefly in a muttered monotone. The A.D.S. looked shrunken; he signed to us. We followed him out. Unbidden, memory of departure in boyhood after caning came welling up. It was good outside. We breathed the free air.

I expect it was about then that we met the M.P. The A.D.S. was now in such extremities of anxiety that he confused us all a little. He was a nice man, probably conscientious, perhaps unwittingly caught in that embarrassment. He took us to the market, so well remembered from the year before; I think it was there we met the M.P. By the store, close to the cassava sellers, we told him all. At once he was as distressed as the A.D.S. He protested passionately that we were not to judge Lukulu on our experience of it—we had been unlucky. They at Lukulu welcomed people from elsewhere; they were anxious to co-operate so that I should see all that I needed to see. After all, I would write in my book about Lukulu and then perhaps people would want to visit it, and in Lukulu they would be glad to welcome tourists. It would be good for Lukulu. He was so ardent and likeable, so concerned to repair what had been done that I felt apologetic for having been ill used.

But for all his anguished helpfulness, and the A.D.S.'s, there was nowhere there we could sleep that night but the bare ground. You sleep thus only when you cannot avoid it. We got into the aeroplane and flew to Mongu. Just like that, I said to myself, remembering my journey to Mongu of a year before, of which I will tell presently. We asked, before we went, if we could expect that the boat would be available next morning. We were told with ferocious certainty that it would. And, next morning when we touched down, there they were to meet us and tell us that the boat was ready. So now, at last—I was to go to the Kabompo confluence. At last I was to see it as Livingstone saw it—and again that memory returned, or what I thought was a memory, that he had gone up-river by boat with a party on shore. But was that all? Was there not something else about that trip? The thought niggled but would not be pinned down.

They took us down to the boat and quite a procession went with us down the abrupt tumble of path through the bananas and mangoes. Men and boys made a privilege of carrying things for us, making such a friendly jollity of it that it sweetened the sour memory of the mission. As momentary pictures will sometimes fix like a stopped frame in a moving picture, I see them still as I saw them then. They stood waving goodbye against the glaucous jungle and the deep blue sky. One young man wore a brilliant pink white-spotted shirt, his protective arm round a little boy in the sky blue shirt. Another wore vermilion, and a Boma messenger looked gay in his pinkish-red and dark blue. There was as much shouting and banter and goodbye-ing as if ours was a departure for unimaginably far places.

We went splendidly at first, bearing up the wide sweep of river with the banks low on either side, thrust by the engine at impressive speed. And that, I thought, is not the way that Livingstone went. In my mind's eye I could see him, in the long dug-out canoe poled by men who so miraculously keep their balance in that outstandingly unstable craft. I was doing it too easily.

So I thought. We bore across the river to follow the far bank, clouding the air with panicking birds, roaring up so fast that we should reach the Kabompo in very little time. We had to pass another confluence first; the Lungwebungu River comes in on the right bank, the one we were following. An island divides the river there and, I remember, I was staring up the inviting entanglement of the creek between island and mainland. We all had our enchanting preoccupations because the river was glorious there, and the morning was lovely.

The shock of impact was immense. We, our gear, everything, were thrown in a tumble over the boat. We were hard aground on rock—but how much and how gripping rock? Were we holed? First the second's stunned blank, then the next one's flooding questioning. The boat was firm, without an inch of roll; we seemed welded to the rock. But no hole, no inflow; we should not sink if we could get off the rock.

By someone's forethought there were oars aboard. We pushed with those, straining till muscles' crack against the rock, but finding all as firm as if we strove to push rock from rock. We could have gone over the side to push the boat, or possibly to lever it with the oars but you do not step carelessly into the Zambezi. You try all other things first. We did get off in the end, with all the weight in the stern and one man forward to push.

We dropped back, eased out to find a channel, questing erratically about the river, peering for clear water. The Kabompo seemed less imminent. Progress was slow, creeping up for a hundred yards or so, finding shoals, dropping back, finding another channel, making a little way and finding rock again. So we went for an hour, with progress less and less till we could find no way. Turn and double as we did, the slabby rock blocked us everywhere. And now I remembered—it came to me what that other supposed memory of Livingstone was. Rightly or wrongly I thought that he, trying up the river as we were, had at last failed to find passage. True or not, I thought even the shallow draught of a canoe could find it impossible. After all I was not to get to the Kabompo.

Dave was comforting—'Let's fly low over it. At least that will be seeing it, won't it? Not the same, I know, but better than not seeing it.'

It was of course. We dropped downstream to navigable water and fished for tiger for a few hours, then got in the aeroplane. Thus, at last, I did see the Kabompo confluence. It is not the best way—seeing from the air, however low-flying, does odd things to scale. It robs dimension to a hardly believable extent. Coming very low over the confluence, the Kabompo looked unmistakably a minor stream compared with the Zambezi. How *could* Livingstone have thought it the main stream? Perhaps it looks drastically different from the ground; perhaps the Zambezi's size is not apparent there; perhaps the Kabompo's is exaggerated. Some time, somehow, I shall have to go back. Livingstone was a very astute geographical observer.

10

It was hot that day. From sunrise it was apparent that the day was
to be like an oven, and its being the rainy season did nothing to
mitigate it; the air was charged with drenching humidity. It would
be hot in Lukulu—on the huge total exposure of the plain we
would broil. And there was to be the maximum chance for heating in the Land Rover; we were to have passengers. A guide for
the plain, Hellmuth said, was essential, and there the guide was.
But not only he; he had friends, several of them climbing with
him into the back. When they were aboard, with them and their
things, and ours, and all that Hellmuth was taking to Mongu, the
vehicle was well filled, almost crammed. Then we were starting,
pulling out from under the mango tree, and others came, several
more for whom it was clear there was no spare inch of room. But
there was shifting in the back, shuffling up, and they climbed in.
The three of us were in the front, and the community of heat and
sweat thickened. However, Land Rovers have merciful flaps which
may be opened above the dash; as we rolled out of Lukulu the
air poured in at least to bring a little cooling to us in front. I suspect that having passed us, it was as limply hot as the rest when it
reached those in the back.

We came out from Lukulu, through the fringe of huts, garden
plots, banana thickets, and then left it all behind. We dropped
down from the last of the higher ground, into the vast lost hot
space of the plain. And lost, I thought, we should certainly be
without the navigation of the guide. We came out on a road, if

such could be called the loose deep trail of dust. Whatever its quality, it was visible. For a few miles it remained so, then began to fade. Near Lukulu, within its ambit, there was traffic enough to the sparse cluster of satellite villages to keep the way marked with usage. But once away into the prostrate vacuum of the plain all that was done. The erstwhile road—and the guide still called it 'the road'—became two precariously traceable wheel-tracks. Sometimes they were quite plainly to be seen, worn free of grass, sometimes they showed as a double flattening of the grass. Sometimes I could see no sign of anything in any direction that gave a hint that there was a difference of orientation anywhere in the whole vast flat circle. Above was the inverted bowl of sky and that had no cloud to show by its movement the wind's direction —and, anyway, there was no breath of wind. Under the sky the encirclement of horizon was unbroken. The tousle of coarse hot grasses grew patchily over the sandy earth and, look which way you would, the straggle of other growth was anonymous—the lean flat-topped thorns, the oil palms, the crouching spiky growths of drought-tolerant plants. All sense of any direction had left me; I had only a general sense of where Lukulu had been because, as I supposed, we were pointing away from it.

I wondered apprehensively if the guide really had any cognizance at all of where we were and where we were headed—how could he in the sun-blasted enigma? But he remained confident, piloting steadily, only occasionally ordering a stop so that he might stand on the tail board to scan ahead. Then his sweep of outstretched arm would direct our course, often bearing to port or starboard, I not being able to see the faintest directional marker. Look which way I would there was the same flat unbroken sea of grass and scrub and lonely palms.

All the distances were uneventful; all, it seemed, was huge sun-drenched vacancy that drained over the horizon to other further horizons that never reached an end. It seemed empty, as landscapes without the least undulation will, and, if you are travelling in a vehicle with its confinement and noise, you are insulated. But when our stops came the sense of hotly teeming life surged upon me. In that endless prostration there was no tussock without its thrum. It could be felt as much as seen; I could hear and sense the burning life. By degrees I perceived that everything was stirring; the ground moved with the million minor and greater lives of every yard. Mostly you do not see the snakes though they are there—once in a while I saw the parting swish of grass, had the moment's sinuous glimpse as a cobra slid away. More often I saw the lizards. Some were large and sensational.

There was one, scuttling away before the Land Rover, startlingly bizarre, almost artificially fanciful. It was a foot long, with a curiously upright stance, raised on its forelegs with its head held high in frozen-postured pauses. Between its sharp slides of movement, stonestill, with its improbable colour, it looked like a contrivance. The light brown of its body was patterned with darker brown, but on head and shoulders and legs it had a hardly possible brilliance of electric blue. It was a gecko, just a common creature, but astonishing at first seeing.

It was odd too that the apparent blanched vacancy of that landscape had a constant flit of birds of such brilliance that they should have been obvious. One would stop, perched for moments, and its flare arrested the eye. Then it would fly and at once was lost. Brilliance, in that blazing light, was more concealing than soberness.

I felt my ignorance. *How* was I to know so many creatures, so many plants, so many trees? By the spending of a life in that one context, I supposed; but, if curiosity is sharp and observations have accumulated in many places, you can detect kinships, or think you can. You note this or that silhouette or mode of flight or characteristic shape and think you see a family connection, and sometimes rightly so. There was a bird that showed recurrently and I, I think mistakenly, identified it with the crows. It *was* slightly crow-like but slim, black on the breast and glitteringly blue elsewhere. I think it may have been of the starlings.

It was during the morning hours that I became aware of a bird much to be seen in Zambia, elsewhere in Africa too, sometimes as much as any other bird. But it is too exquisite to be called common, though it is ubiquitous; rather it should be said to haunt the country. Perhaps that *is* sentimentalizing; perhaps I should admit the bird is common. But the house sparrow is common and so are many other mundane things. The carmine bee-eater could not shake off its air of precious rarity if it perched on every roof—but of course you do not, nor ever would, see such a creature in such circumstances. Nature does not devise it so. The bird belongs to lonely wilderness.

I saw its shimmer solidify when it alighted on the scrub as we paused and veered to find direction. Suddenly out of the spangled air it was there, almost within touch. All bee-eaters are beautiful, but their beauty culminates in the carmine one. It is bigger than the rest as, being perfect, it can afford to be. It has the upright slenderness of its kind, the long dark curving beak, and the tail, always fancifully fine in the bee-eaters, is prolonged into two slender pencilled points. But how *can* the colour be conveyed? Detail that, but there is still the miracle of its texture and flirting with the light. For what it may convey, the top of the head is intense turquoise blue and so are the under-coverts of the tail. Throat and breast are pure sheer carmine, back and wings a mingling of carmine and ruddy-red. Those are the colours. But the bird *burns*. It is illuminated. Recurrently through that day's eternity it was with us, materializing for moments then vanishing back into the air from which it had crystallized.

Hours had gone since, now hardly to be remembered, we had left Lukulu. We were swallowed by the immensity of the plain, negated by it—so, as it seemed, removed from human life, that things beyond that inviolable horizon were too tenuous for belief. By the sun I knew it to be the latter part of morning, but time had no shape; for time to have shape, as I now discovered, it must have a context of changing forms. The invincible circle of land under the perpetually burning dome of sky was without form. Hour follows hour and there is no slightest change; it induces numbness. Even our guide was hesitant now, calling more often for navigational stops, scanning blank distances then flinging a directive arm with apparent confidence. I hoped ardently that it was justified. It was easy to imagine a future of endless pursuit of that horizon. On such African journeyings of a day (if all goes well) you do not take food; food is at journey's end and, already, that seemed unbelievably distant.

It was about midday that the port distance showed a tiny tuft. It enlarged and became the slightest lifting into a low mound grown with trees, and my eyes were grateful for it. Kay had no sense of denial of altitudes; she was in a dream of return. She was born on the plain. Our course as set would have left the place on our beam but we diverged partly to seek re-direction, but as much because there was a settlement there, a minute village. Where man was so rare an animal it was impossible to pass without communication.

There were low walls as we approached the village, earthen banks two to three feet high running some hundred yards each way out from the mound and making an enclosure. When the rains come, Kay said, the flood will take over all this land to the eye's limit, and only the village will stand just above the water. Then about April, or May perhaps, the water will go back, returning to the river and leaving dry land again on the plain. But within the earth-walled enclosure the water will be trapped and with it the fish. That will be valuable protein for the village.

And the mound itself is man-made, Kay said as we came to it. At intervals over the plain there are these tiny nodules of humanity, each one raised just so high that it will be an island when the whole plain is a sea. That, I thought, seeing it even when the plain was dry, is an almost inconceivable loneliness. We passed an old man working with the traditional hoe among the maize. He was wearing a loin garment with a flap hanging in front and another behind and he raised his lean frame slowly to rest on his hoe and stare at us. He said nothing and made no gesture, and seemed to be seeing us as something half remembered. But he was old; who knows for what total of dry and rainy seasons he had been lost in the centre of that emptiness?

It was different with those in the village. They met us, the children surrounding the Land Rover before it had stopped, smiling with shy eagerness. They offered their little black-backed pink palmed hands for shaking. The older people, men and women, smiling and welcoming, brought us the small, very sweet bananas that grow there. The sense of the place was what I supposed an oasis must be, though then I had never been to one. It was as if all was turned inwards from the enormous loneliness that lapped it, walled and domed by its growth—lofty great-boled eucalyptus, dense thicketing of bananas. The people, in the way of very isolated people, were ingenuously friendly. The children, wearing nothing but a minimal strip at their middles, were confiding, quickly affectionate. They, and the adults, looked into our eyes with utter openness, as if through them you could look into the backs of their souls. We stayed for a while there, in the central space where press of feet had given a satiny polish to the ground, talking and shaking hands until, having been directed, it was time to go. They waved and were sad and then we were absorbed by space again and the village had become lost in the sunny swim of distance.

There might be difficulty, they had said. Though it was early in the rainy season, before the flood would engulf the world, the water had begun to accumulate in places. The least hollow on our way could have turned to a morass; and so we found it. A few miles beyond the village the track, at this point just visible, dropped down a slight incline. 'Stop', the guide said, and he went forward to tread cautiously in the hollow. It was soft, so infirmly water-filled that even the Land Rover could not have found passage. We fanned out, spreading and feeling with our feet to find firm ground, finding nothing but the same spongy yielding. For all practical distance to either side of the way ahead there was no possibility of passage. 'Turn,' the guide said, 'we must go back, we must find a long way round', and when we were nearly back at the village on its mound he directed us off on a tangent to starboard. It seemed haphazard and no more than hopeful guessing, but presently there was a track again—or that faint suggestion of one that I had begun to be able to detect.

We went on, losing the trail, finding it, traversing the miles but with no effective progress because every mile appeared the same as the one preceding it—rather as if we drove on a revolving band. Only Kay, probably, was contentedly absorbed, recognizing, identifying, remembering. 'You see that plant,' she said, 'the spiky one? It's wild sisal.'

It grew in clumps, particularly in the shadow of the thorn trees, stiff half-organic-looking plants, tubular and matt or eggshell-textured, light cool green, each rigid leaf terminating in a lance-sharp point. It had its many uses, its fibres serving all sorts of purposes. But not as many, Kay said, as the low-growing fan-like palm that made dense clumps in every direction—so common a plant indeed, not only here but almost anywhere in open bush, that I took it for granted. It was the best source of material for basketry and Kay's people, the Lozi, are great basket makers. Her grandmother, Kay said, had taught her, showing her how to take out the heart of the plant and boil it till its tough fibres could be had. They made the very finest sorts of basket, either natural or dyed—and Lozi basketry has much decorative patterning with weavings of different colours. These very strong heart fibres are also used for the fine but strong tyings needed in the joining of one part to another in baskets. The leaves give strips for basket making too, but not of such quality as the heart; that makes the very best and strongest baskets. Before they can be used the fibres must be soaked to make them workable—used dry they are brittle.

'My grandmother showed me how to weave the strips and make the patterns, as every generation teaches another; and she taught me pottery too. I learnt how to build the shape of the pot with coils of clay and then, when it was utterly dry, not a bit before, how to fire it. We would dig a pit in the ground and put the pot in it, and then fill the pot with carbon and pack it round with carbon too till the pit was tightly filled. Then over that we would make a fire, a big fire, and it was always made of dried cow dung because that would burn slowly and at just the right temperature to fire the pot without cracking it. A wood fire would have been too quick and fierce. The fire would be allowed to burn right out, until it was quite dead and entirely without any kindling. Even then we would wait, not touching the pot until it had cooled completely.'

We came then, as Kay told me of these crafts, to another village on its mound, so minute a place that there seemed to be only a dozen or so people there and only the merest cluster of very simple huts. One was just a roof and three walls, its open front hung with a woven mat.

'That,' said Kay, 'is made as I said with fibres from that palm —but the work—it is not good. My grandmother would not have allowed me to do work like that. The weave of it is not close enough and regular enough.'

It was the hottest time of day now and perhaps that was why this place had none of the happiness of the previous one. Perhaps it was that or perhaps it was too tiny and lost in that infinity even for those bred to it. They seemed negatived; their eyes looked as if they no longer saw, and though we now found each movement hampered by the heat's pressure there seemed in them a deeper ennui. They talked to us in a desultory way as if neither pleased nor displeased that we had come. There was an air of lost movement in the place and, I remember, at the edge of the mound there grew a sausage tree. I noticed how utterly still it was, how each heavy composite leaf hung without stirring and, anyway, the tree has a look of heavy hanging. The fruits are long, sausage-shaped, quite two feet long and weighing as much as nine pounds. This tree still bore the last of its blossoms, great velvet tubes of deep crimson, but sumptuous as they are it is the fruits that impress. As so often in Africa on the first seeing of animals or plants or trees, you cannot quite believe it. There is no difficulty in believing that bark and fruit from the tree are used mysteriously in the rites of the witch doctors. The queer oddity of the tree is suggestive enough of that. *MuZungula* they call it there in the Lozi country, though I think the Bemba name, *muFungufungu,* has more of the sense of it. When it grows anywhere near a river you will always find the ground well printed with the tread of hippo, because they (and rhino, squirrels, mongeese and monkeys) are inordinately fond of the fruits. Humans, knowing the ways of the tree, avoid its shelter; one of its fruits dropped on the head is far from being the joke it might seem to be.

I was looking at it, and I think I had fallen into a state of heat-bemused vacancy, that and the feeling of the place, when I saw far away across the sea of land a dark pencil standing from earth to heaven. It advanced at high speed growing and showing till I saw that it was a whirling funnel, small-pointed at the bottom and coning narrowly to its wider top many hundreds of feet high. It was a whirlwind, spinning and travelling at astonishing speed. In moments or little more it came from its far distance to pass half a mile or so wide of the village. No one looked at it, no one commented. Their languid eyes looked at nothing and saw nothing.

We left them, going on again towards the ever-receding meeting of sky and land. For all the change there was in the hot quiver of that vista we might have been rolling in a vast circle and I might have thought we were had I not, from time to time, faintly discerned the track in what was so nearly trackless. Not a glimpse of the river had we had since leaving Lukulu, but the birds were a sign that our course was approximately that of the river. Once there was a fish eagle; skeins of geese scored occasional lines across the sky. There was a great event each year, Kay said, when she was a child. It was called *Sitaka*; it was seeing the geese made her remember it.

'It came each year at the time when the birds were nesting in great hosts in the forests of reeds by the river. There were geese and duck and all sorts of water fowl and birds that love the river. Everybody went then to catch them, men and women, and the children. Some used fish spears and some used just their hands, grabbing them. For two weeks everyone, absolutely everyone of every age ate birds—it was a grand festival you see, a festival of poultry. Though women and children went to the river, really it was something for the men—all of them went, all together getting birds so that there were so many that only a small part of them could be eaten then, in all that feasting. There were *huge* numbers of birds. Most of them, really, had to be preserved. Many were cooked very slowly in salt water, not too much salt, and then they would be sun-dried to make biltong. That made a store of food that could be used whenever it was needed, all over the year. It was very practical of course, but that wasn't the spirit of it. Really it was a great festival of the year. Everybody looked forward to it, and everybody had a high festival spirit all through the two weeks of it.'

The change came imperceptibly. When I had lost expectation

of an end and had fallen into acceptance of the horizon's perpetual imprisonment of us, I saw that the track was becoming positive, discernible a distance ahead. There was more evidence of man, herds of cattle, several tiny villages on their mounds.

We stopped by one, waiting while the guide inquired for the destination of one of our passengers, which was thought to be in the vicinity. We stood by the Land Rover, using its shade and sweating in the freedom of the air, loosening the wet cling of clothes.

Our passenger's destination was near the river. We came suddenly to the bank, not seeing the water until we swung out of the high grass and stopped above it.

'You will wait here while I take this man, *ja*?' Hellmuth asked, and when he had gone and the Land Rover's sound had sunk into distance, we were in an enormous aloneness, inconspicuous as ants in that gargantuan levelness. The weather had changed, a pale flat suffusion covering the sky and putting a white light on everything, flattening further what was utter flatness. The land lay unbroken to the horizon and from our feet to the far bank, so far and so low that it was a slim line, the river was a still shimmer flatly reflecting the white glaze of the sky. There were cattle there, hundreds of beasts dark and tiny and distant like a stipple. There were sounds, the geese's voices and the waders' piping, the frogs in the reed forests. But all that was muted by the huge hollow of the place, everything hushed. We were hushed too, as if we had no mandate to speak. So we stayed, silently until the Land Rover returned.

There had been re-direction from the village and soon there was sense of the proximity of Mongu. We bore away from the river on the now well-marked track because Mongu lies not by the river but inland from it, receiving its waters by a system of canals. It is situated so for the advantage of a lift of ground that gives it immunity from the flood of the wettest rainy season. The weather had changed further; a storm was coming. No sun showed now, no light; the high white screen of cloud had been overcome by a lowering roll of darkness. The air had become heavy, as if with the weight of the indigo mass above. Puffs of wind came, suddenly out of utter stillness, pushing the supine air against us for a moment and dying. Everything lay waiting. It grew darker; the only light a low glitter on the distant world's rim. The rest was night, blue-black. The first raindrops fell, spaced out, thickened, came together, solid. We were in the blind midst of it, a roaring vertical solidity of water. Wind had come and that roared too, and then all was crushed flat by the rending violence of thunder. Hellmuth drove on, feeling with the headlights, picking momentary glimpses of track which seemed to slew and slither, though it was we who skidded. The lightning came intermittently and its blue blaze entangled with the falling water so that it blinded us. Lakes were forming, the track had gone—we drove where the grass did not show above the water, doing that anyway in the fragments of visibility; the wave we threw joined in blinding our way ahead.

It had come very suddenly after first warning and for half an hour it raged, then, as if by a switch, it stopped. The rain ceased and the wind dropped; there was no lightning and no thunder. There was nothing but a beatific silence and stillness. The air was light and wetly fresh. Then the sun thrust through like a vast bright hand and pushed away the darkness. Everything shone in sun-reflecting glitter. The water sank and vanished as we watched. Soon the track was dry, kiln-dry again. It takes a long persistent deluge before the dry earth is filled and ready to flood.

It was close to evening now; there would be little more of the light. The sun rides high by day and at evening it goes down with no slow decline or mystery of twilight. The abrupt fall to darkness was not far off and we searched ahead for sight of Mongu. It

131

showed first as a slight thickening of the severe fine line of the horizon, became a blob and then a shallow hump and that was Mongu, taking form and stature. It was not a very high eminence, but almost dramatic in its contrast with the illimitable level about it. Right to the outskirts we continued on the track in the sea of grass; then, as if the plain beleaguered the place, it rose suddenly, as if defensively. We passed in a moment from the flat wild waste to a made-up road winding into the slope that climbed the town. Almost at the top there is a little hotel, wonderful to find there, with a bar and a terrace and lounging chairs, a place with the incredible luxuries of proper meals and sprung beds in real bedrooms. But first we had to part from Hellmuth.

He leapt from the Land Rover, began to swing out our gear.

'You will pay me now, *ja*?' and he named a sum which I have forgotten but which was ample. But we have to get to the airfield in the morning, we told him, quite a long way. Could we not leave our gear in the Land Rover overnight, and then he, perhaps, would drive us out?

He was putting the money away. 'You will walk to the airfield, *ja*?'

But our gear, we said, what can we do about that?

'You will walk several times and carry it, *ja*?' He got into the Land Rover and let in the clutch. We never saw him again.

We looked at each other. Agreement needed no speech. That was tomorrow's problem. Tonight there was beer and food and comfort.

Kay talked as we sat with the beer, nostalgically remembering her childhood there with her father, who was a teacher, and her mother. She talked of the Litunga too, her relative, and of the great state attaching to his office. Its original royal rank is reduced now to Paramount Chief but some of the old grandeur remains. Particularly so at the annual ceremonial called *Kuomboka*, which is that of the transference from the dry season residence to that of the rainy season. The dry season one is at Lealue and it lies low, between Mongu and the river. In March when the water rises over the plain Lealue must be evacuated. The move is made to Limulunga, on higher ground and inviolate. The journey is stately, made in the state canoe, a great vessel by the standard of its kind, very long and painted with broad vertical stripes of black and white. At its midships there is a large domed canopy for the proper sheltering of the Litunga's dignity. The crew is packed in, shoulder to shoulder for the length of the boat, all driving paddles with long tapering handles spirally painted. They wear a traditional costume—a rather turban-like red cap with a wicker coronet holding a high feather tuft, and a wrapped skirt of printed cotton.

Between dawn and sunrise in the morning I stood at the edge of the eminence above the plain. The land lay away like a sea in petrified calm, utterly flat, unrippled. Yet, I thought, that hardly conceivable level is not lowland. It is between 3,000 and 4,000 feet above sea level. What moment of catastrophic frenzy could have produced *that* uplift? The one perhaps that rent apart the whole continent to make the great Rift Valley that runs most of the north and south length of Africa. But in whatever cosmic uproar it was made, the plain had an enormous serenity now in the early slant of light. It looked empty of everything, a huge forgetfulness of space. But life was there. Its human part was thinly scattered, all those lonely knots of Barotse people, all looking to Mongu as their centre. In their differing ways they come to Mongu, getting stores and returning, and many come by the river.

As you come down the river from Lukulu to Mongu you see the little shanty places, temporary-looking huts set up on sand spits and banks. There are always people there and they offer hospitality over the night to those who make slow way poling up from Mongu.

133

Kay and I, later, walked through Mongu looking for means of transport to the airfield. We met a large and friendly Scot whom we shall never see again. He lent us a Land Rover and a driver and would take nothing for that.

11

At Senanga we were met by the District Governor and the District Secretary; they were a gift of providence to expunge the memory of Lukulu. The District Governor was tall and had a cast in one eye which gave him, as it sometimes may, a very winning look of benevolence. The benevolence nevertheless was real, and the District Secretary was as warmly full of it. He was as cosily tiny and round as the D.G. was tall. The welcome of the two of them, lanky and little, was so gently and quietly friendly that I have remembered it photographically, as if the sunlit picture of it stands framed and held forever in the snapped moment. There is the D.G. straight with legs together and feet a little splayed, with head sideways inclined and his smile enhanced by his errant eye. And there is the D.S., rather light coloured, cocoa wood softly polished, slightly leaning forward, faintly shy and faintly eager. The background is the town, open and spacious and rising slightly away and seen between the bare and twisting limbs of trees. That was the fixed moment, and then the action runs on, the charming small ceremony of welcome, and the D.S. bearing us away in his Land Rover.

He took us to the rest house and that, with our past's conditioning, was benign revelation. So soon I had begun to feel that a beatitude lay on Senanga. Nothing subsequently lessened that feeling. I am experienced in rest houses; I know the span of their quality. The rest house at Senanga has its own fond and separate niche of remembrance. It stood on nearly the highest ground of the shallow rise that Senanga has from the plain, U-shaped and enclosing a pretty neatness of garden with a pawpaw and flowers and some succulent shrubs in which there was often a chameleon performing its miracles. From the garden and from the verandah the prospect had a serenity. The ground declined easily to the water, two or three hundred yards away, a great sky-reflecting horseshoe tranquillity, flanked with groves of trees to the one side and to the other the still immensity of the plain, calmly quiet in the evening light. There had been so lean and rough and hard a time from the far source to here that I seemed to have come to the tranquil heaven that is said to follow travail. I, who had been sceptical about that, told myself that just sometimes so it may be.

From that reverie I was brought by the D.S. His fund of revelation was not exhausted.

'Down there,' he said, pointing down the broad way under the trees which fell away from the rest house, 'down there we have a bar, a very nice bar. Perhaps you would like to come there soon?'

So—that too. All this and Lukulu in one world.

'But come—you will want to see your rooms and meet the staff and then, yes eat something? Then we will go to the bar.'

The staff were three. The cook was as tall and thin and bendy from top to bottom as an angularly jointed grass stem, lined and smoke-seamed from attendance upon the wood burning range in the kitchen. We met him there, and the others, and he, aproned and bearing a cooking slice like a sceptre, received us with courtesy, offering us the freedom of the place with bowing inclinations and wide and easy gestures. In very little time he produced a meal of eggs and bread and something else and we ate it quickly to be ready for the D.S. who waited to conduct us to the bar.

The day had gone now, and in soft first dark of evening we went out down the broad dust way under the trees, not able to see but hearing the murmuring of those going that way too, and the fragments of laughter and the high sudden voices of the

136

women. The multiple shuffle in the dust suggested that the bar was a well-shared objective.

It proclaimed itself ahead of our coming. Its flare of light slashed a space in the darkness; the noise bulged into the night. Light and sound engulfed us as we walked the verandah and came to the door. The juke box was inside, in the first room, louder than I had known a juke box could be. For the first moments, out of still starlight, that and the strident gush of life were overwhelming. The bar counter was in the first room and they were dancing there with a curious privacy in the stunning blast of light and sound. Some had paired, girl to girl, man to man, but most had their private worlds, lathy young men and shuffling youths, barefoot in one place. They writhed subduedly with lolling heads and unseeing eyes and some solitary girls squirmed privately. Because their head scarves were so low over their eyes they peered blankly with back-tilted heads like guardsmen. Their dancing was partly in the traditional manner with drooping trunks and fidgeting buttocks, but crossed with modern jives and jerks and quivers.

We threaded through two rooms beyond, divided by waist-high walls. There were chairs and tables there, thronged and noisy, the whole place a merry rowdy roar. They made space for us and the ear adjusted and conversation became possible. Possible and obligatory; no cool frontiers of non-acquaintance to thaw and fall in the stilted fashion of the West. We were taken in, absorbed, those with us engaging us, others coming to speak with the soft handclap of greeting and slight stooping of the knees. Sometimes they had English and sometimes they had not and sometimes I was not quite sure. They spoke their way and I spoke mine, and we got on comfortably enough with no particular misunderstanding if, often, not much understanding either.

The girl brought the beer. She was black and strapping and

lovely. Her belted overall was pressed and white, and she made it voluptuous, going with the beat and balancing the tray and sliding through with rhythms shivering in shoulders and hips and nodding head. A crown opener hung at her waist; she opened the bottles at the table and made that seem erotic. Most she did with a brief and practised flick but where her fancy lay she put slow fingers caressingly round the bottle top, with heavy black-eyed glancing under her lids. She had a high voice, rather syncopated, like a tinkling on hollow wood.

We drank from the bottle, as is the African way, and there is a knack to that. You use lips and tongue so that the beer flows easily and you do not choke or get air locks in the bottle neck. When the empties accumulated and the tables were forested with them, the company called the girl and she came with dignity. She conveyed the sense of a favour hardly deserved, but signalled exception to her fancy.

They asked me whence I had come, and when I told them I had been at the source and had walked through the Ndembu country a deep pleasure suffused the D.S.

'That is my home—that is where I come from, and my wife too. We are Ndembu. But I expect you do not know our village where we were born and grew up. I don't expect you know Nkomba village.'

Nkomba village! Nkomba where they had bathed in the stripling river among the rocks, where the first bridge was a log cage filled with rocks. Nkomba where we had been that heat-riven day when we tottered into Mwinimilambo and had honey beer with Chief Mwinimilambo.

All present shared the pleasure of this emotional discovery, and when the girl brought the bottles for the toasting of it she conveyed a richly tender favour.

So happy did the evening become that I lost sense of its uproar. We became a very united company, and there seemed nothing odd when the woman came so portentously to stand over me. She was very solemn. She insisted upon shaking hands with everyone of us within reach and it seemed very significant. I think she was going to be oracular. But the man next to me stood and fixed her with a severe eye, so oddly inhibiting her that she stood submissively as he harangued her. I know the general sense of his oration because he repeated every word of it to me afterwards. Everyone in Zambia, he said, must look forward. No one must look back. No one must allow anyone else to look back. There must be a universal going forward in a spirit of equality. There was more, much more, but all on that theme. I wondered what omission of social responsibility had made the woman such a target. Or perhaps she was a chance convenience for what was bursting for egress. She attempted no defence but stayed submissively while the downpour of his reproof continued, as if caught without an umbrella and already too wet for defence. The bonhomie of the evening flagged. He was, they told me, Secretary of the Rural District Council, or some sort of African equivalent.

It was not till next morning that I met the Professor and, though he was not a professor, it is only so that I shall ever be able to think of him. I had wakened early, just as the first abrupt spears of sunlight blazed up from the horizon, lifting the quickly climbing sun. I was early but not early enough not to lag. Senanga was awake and tinkling with morning life, happily meeting another day; and yes, I said to myself, Senanga is a happy place. I watched from the window, and the women carrying water and the children and everyone going on the broad way between the massy trees laughed and walked with a sort of gaiety. It was lovely there too, with the dusty avenue making a fine vista down to where the bar lay just out of sight, the road lying in the sun and the shade heavy under the trees. In the kitchen the slants of sun spangled the dust, wood smoke from the range lay aromatically and the cook made courtly movements with his cooking slice as he invited us to have eggs for breakfast.

We had hardly finished them when the driver came, and I took him to be something quite other and far more grand than a driver because he was tall, immaculate, and had an air. He had something of a presence, with his rather handsome face and slim fine figure in elegantly pressed whites. He ushered us, so to speak, and there was the Land Rover.

At the Boma there was a green sward and all was spacious with the same gaiety as by the rest house, but with just the touch of firm formality that conveyed authority. The trees stood widely spaced, the mauve haze of jacaranda and the flaming of the flamboyants, and the Boma building lay in the dapple under them. The smartly saluting police and Boma messengers were splendid in shiningly ironed uniforms, and I thought again as I had often thought before that the skin of their legs between shorts and puttees had a bloom, like that on the skin of a ripe purple-black plum.

The D.S. was in his room, and when he had taken us to the D.G. already the lot of us were like a happy meeting of friends. Everyone smiled, the small jokes crackled, and they told us about the Professor. No one but the Professor could tell me all the things I would like to know about that country and its people; only he knew all the lore and the stories, and his talk, they said, was like the reading of a great book. He would be coming soon because they had told him about what I sought to see and learn; he would give as much of his time as I wanted.

He came in bustling and amiable and, it seemed to me, with an eagerness for such an exceptionally appreciative recipient for all the learning that burnt in him. He was a little man, on the elderly side, wrinkled and seamed, but very lively, suggesting a very active and rather sweetly friendly prune. His talk began at once, the words slipping and tumbling along rather softly and quietly like the running of a small stream among the stones. He took me over, determined that no shred of his store should not be put out for my use. All that country, right down past Nangweshi, down to the great falls, to Livingstone's tree, all that he would show me, and as he showed me he would tell me all that he had learned about all these places in all the years he had been living there— and for all his long life he had been there, on the plain and down to the forests below. If I would continue at Senanga for a while— and the D.S. and the D.G. added their smiling pressure upon me to do so—we could make many expeditions and he would tell of the people and places.

We went out of Senanga now, going downstream, due south, across the southern end of the Barotse Plain and again, for a moment, a sense of lonely immensity swept over me. This was, I suppose, as near the centre of Africa as you can be, a thousand miles from the nearest sea, but especially on the Barotse Plain there is the sense of it—a pervasive sense of lostness, of remoteness from all else. How, I wondered, would it seem, being alone in this trap of infinity, and I thought again of Livingstone as I so constantly did. I, in a vehicle, with the knowledge of a safe base for return, felt the weight of the loneliness. I was inoculated against the inherent diseases of the places, I had my pills against malaria and I went established ways. For Livingstone there was nothing. He went where no white man had been, vulnerable to everything, with no base but where he stopped.

Our way was not uncharted as his was, we went on a road which, if not smooth, at least had points of departure and arrival. It was *not* smooth; it was very rough indeed, but being called, as it was, the best road in Western Province, suggested privilege. We could be much worse off.

Spaced along the way there were posts, twisty and nobbled, like lean men, each painted with a white mark. They marked maximum flood heights, and with some at fully fifteen feet they were impressive. The road was at least that height above present river level, probably much more; so great a mass of water, so immeasurably spread, baulked the imagination when the plain lay there as flatly hot as a brick from the kiln. There had been a change early in the century—for whatever reason flooding had become more severe, surmounting minor heights previously inviolate.

For three miles or so the road went and then came to a ferry. The road turned abruptly, went back on itself and dropped steeply on the raw red of its recent excavation to reach the water's edge. The ferry vessel was loading by the distant far bank and so, with the idling few already there, we must wait. It was quiet; distantly I heard the faint shrillness of a fish eagle and other sounds fell singly. In the tremor of heat the women with their huge head burdens, and the squatting men, stared sightlessly over the river. I wandered back from the river, threading through the scrub and yellow straggles of grass to where rangy cattle sought a living in the charge of three small boys. They were picturesque, these beasts, lean as mountain goats—and I thought it nearly miraculous that they sustained life at all on what I could see—and bizarrely marked, red and white and black and white, patched and spotted and crazily skewbald, some like Dalmatian dogs. But spindly as they were they had some distinction from the splendour of their horns, five and six feet across, with a fine fierce sweep, though the creatures were as harmlessly tame as sheep, and probably, on that diet, with no bit of energy to spare for ferocity. I must have been regarding them over-intently and, to the boys, inexplicably for something so ordinary; they, the boys, ranged themselves between the cattle and me and danced and pranced, pulled faces and hollered.

The ferry came, a ponderous grey crawling thing with a thick oily smell and a grumble of engines, and we in the Land Rover went aboard and the Professor talked. I asked him how, in Lozi my journey could be described because, some time, I must find a title for this book and that might lead me to one. What I had undertaken could, he said, be described by the word *lieto*—'It means "stranger's journey", and you are making a stranger's journey down the Zambezi—you could say "*Lieto nwanuka ya Zambezi*", or "*Lieto mwa Zambezi*", which means "Journey down the Zambezi".

'But do not suppose,' he said, 'that because we all speak Lozi, the Lozi are the only tribe in the Barotse country. Just in the Senanga District there are these tribes—Quandi, Simaa, Shangao, Yeyi, Mafwe, Totela, Quangwa, Mbunda, Chokwe, a few Luvale, and the Mashi people—all those as well as the Lozi.'

Sitoto was the village on the other bank, the western one; we drove ashore there and, turning south, went on through the last part of the plain before forested land rises away from it.

'Here it is called the Matabele Plain,' the Professor said, 'and there is a good reason for that. You have heard of the Matabele? They were a fierce people, a terror to all the tribes. They used to come raiding up from the south and even now the name is something to make you tremble. But the Kololo were here then, and they were great fighting people too and clever as well. They had also come from the south, from what is now Botswana, and had conquered a lot of the Barotse country, driving back the Lozi. They had made a capital at Sesheke, down-river from here, so as to be able to stop the Matabele raiding into the Barotse country; then here, just here on this Matabele Plain, they had a great victory. You see the Matabele were on this bank, the western one, and looking over the river from here you see what looks like the east bank. But it is not really—it is Mbeta Island, the biggest island on the Zambezi. The Matabele did not know that.

'The Kololo were on the east bank and, very privately, they put some cattle on the island, including a cow without her calf. Of course the cow called and called for her calf until the calf swam over to the island—without being taken by a crocodile. The Matabele heard the cow, saw that there were cattle, and just supposed that there was the east bank, and that there they could raid deeply into the Kololo's territory. The whole army of them went over in canoes, on to the island. The Kololo waited till night. Then they stole over from the real east bank and took away the canoes. Then they sat down and waited. When time had passed, some weeks, and the Matabele were starving, they crossed to the island and killed them all. That was the end of trouble with the Matabele.'

As I knew, and I think it was Kay who had told me, subsequently the Lozi regained their lost hold on the Barotse Plain, pushing the Kololo back to their country south of the Zambezi. But there had been much intermingling of culture and of blood, and I think Kay, not only Lozi but also royal Lozi, considered herself to have much Kololo in her.

'It is also called the Sipo Plain,' the Professor went on, 'and the battle with the Matabele is not the only thing which has given it fame. There were the witch doctors too.'

'Why—was this a place for witch doctors?'

'Oh yes, they were sent here you see. It was full of witch doctors and their sons and daughters—but of course, you do not know how that was. You see when a man was pointed out as a witch doctor he was killed, always; he was burnt alive. Then the first missionaries came to Barotseland, as it was then, and they heard of this and saw it, and they went to the Litunga. This is wrong, they told him; sometimes these men are not witch doctors but someone is their enemy. Can you not find a place to send them instead of killing them? The Litunga listened. He decreed that in future they should be sent to the Sipo Plain, and so they came from everywhere over the Barotse Plain—from Mongu, from Kalabo which is away north of here and west of the river, from Senanga, and they were in peace.'

A leper, near Lukulu

The author with tiger fish, Lukulu

'Do they still come here?'

'Ah no. Gradually the sending of them stopped because it was made to be against the law to point out a man as a witch doctor. To do so meant gaol.'

Passing southward out of the Matabele Plain we had come, at last, to the end of the great Barotse Flood Plain, that vast spacious world-within-a-world whose captives we had been from Lukulu down.

The ground rose, only slightly, but enough to make utter change from the enormity of levelness and inviolate horizons to the north. Here, at once, it was forest, hugely stretching away with nothing else at all, on the west bank anyway, all the way down to Katima Mulilo. The colonnades of great boles and the sun-lanced alleys between would have had a splendour whatever the season, but now the coming of the rains had brought an exuberance of leaf bursting through the boughs. At every slight rise there was the vista of the wider and wider Zambezi, no longer smoothly shining, but going in a white cataract, with the limitless forest rolling to the horizon.

We went down past Nangweshi, a sparse straggle in the hold of the forest and on to Sioma which, largely, is a mission that, as usually happens, had gathered about it a village. A store was there, and thither we went because it was well on in the morning now and hot and we needed beer. The children played in the dust by the steps and men, lazy in the heat, filled the verandah's shade. It was dim and relatively cool inside and the smell, the familiar unforgettable smell of the African village store, absorbed us. I sniffed it gratefully—the mingling of cereals, mostly maize, of trodden boards, cassava, cotton bales, sacking and sweat. I cannot dissociate the smell from the cool bliss of bottled beer in the day's heat.

Outside two very small boys dressed in nothing but dust and ragged shorts smiled at me shyly. The only coins in my pocket were a one-Ngwee piece and a five-Ngwee piece, which is very close to nothing at all. But they accepted them, one each, with solemn politeness. They were in the charge of a big sister, all of five years old and very careful of them. She took charge of the money, indicating that they were a little young for the responsibility of it. I stroked the harshly kinky pate of one and the other came to put his head too for the stroking; and both came again, smiling confidingly and offering their heads. I tickled the rotund tummy of one and, at once, was coerced to tickle the other. The older one might have been a bit upwards of three.

We went south again because, the Professor said, the great falls were further down the river, not far, and indeed they were usually called the Sioma Falls. They have another name, the one given them on the maps, Ngonye Falls, but it is not the one most often used.

'Livingstone knew the Sioma Falls, Bwana,' the Professor told me, 'he used to go to them to look at them, and they are very good to look at, as you will see. Livingstone was much about this district—over there, on the other bank, but downstream some miles there is a tree which I will show you one day. Livingstone would sit under it, by himself, looking for hours at the river going by. It is very wide there and wild and rough among the rocks before, not very much further down, it goes over the Sioma Falls.'

There were salt springs not far from the falls, welling up just in from the road, white-caked at the sides and salt-tasting on the fingertip. Going on from there, ducking under the trees and scrambling down among the rocks, we came suddenly upon the gorge. The huge litter of rocks, as if gargantuanly tossed, were the walls; at the bottom the monstrous thrash of water poured through, fighting the rocks' constriction. Some hundreds of yards upstream I could see falls framed by the mountainous stacking of rock.

'No, Bwana—don't sit; snakes you know. There are many among the rocks.'

That I could imagine, looking at them, so many crevicy havens for snakes. But these were curious rocks, not mere stone, not granite or limestone or sandstone or anything of such familiar kind. They were yellow mostly, richly amber and shining, with a translucent glow of colour and of an odd texture. It reminded me of frog spawn, or tapioca, largely granular, apparently a conglomerate of up to pea-size spherical crystal units. There were some a deep vinous red.

We worked up towards the falls, picking teetering footholds, and I realized that the impression of an enormous tossing of the rocks was not just a visual effect. Little moss or lichen had found purchase on the stones—I could see that they were too briefly settled in one order for that and I could imagine how the godlike violence of the floods of each rainy season tossed them. The litter stacked up from the water was loose and looked temporary, though some of the stones were half the size of a house.

At the top, near the fall, I could see that the gorge was only one of a labyrinth, and that the fall, great as it was, was one of a series with a vista of spray-piles to a distance that could not be less than a mile. I was to qualify that estimate later; I was to admit that the river's width there was no less than the mile and a quarter of the Victoria Falls, and I think it was more. Opposite the near fall, at the point of an island between two gorges, a Land Rover lay shattered on the rocks.

'Yes,' said the Professor, looking at it. 'That is how it has always been. Three hundred years ago a party of the Mbowe people came down the river in their boats and were caught in the powerful stream above the biggest fall. They were swept over to be smashed to pieces among the rocks.'

I thought that if I had never seen the Victoria Falls I would think this the most majestically impressive river falls of all, and, looking at the boiling interlacing of currents in the gorge, I thought of Livingstone coming upon it with his newly wondering eyes—because, I believe, he was the first white man ever to see it. He, with eyes laden with the weariness of months of torrid bush marching, must have come unsuspecting upon the majesty of this sight. The sight was in its way, to me at least, more impressive than the Victoria Falls. The Victoria Falls are frequented. Mighty and dramatic as they are the wildness has gone. The Sioma Falls are far, far from anywhere; they are there in the wild, unvisited, on this lost wilderness of river between Senanga and Sesheke where no one comes. We, probably, were the first to put foot by the river there for a long time; and who would come after us and how soon? It was utterly lonely, utter wilderness.

12

Back in Sioma it was past two o'clock and we were hungry. African village stores yield no luxury but we were able to buy canned sausages, corned beef and, inevitably, baked beans. Go to the house of the man who owns the store, they said, ask him to let you have the food in his house; and, when we went there, it was he who came to the door opening on to the verandah under the scramble of blossom. Would he be so kind as to let us eat in his house, to have the food in our cans warmed and put out? He was a big man, not tall, but heavy, with wide hanging shoulders and slight corpulence, about fifty. He wore a crumpled shirt and old dark trousers and was stubbled on the face but he had the air of a prince, easy and gracious. Yes, of course, he would be delighted for us to use his house for our meal—please to regard it and all he had as being at our service, and he took us in and sat us round the pitch-pine boarded entrance hall. While we waited he made slow conversation, asking us politely about ourselves.

We were summoned soon by his wife, conducted to another room where our food was set out. It was to be a *nshima* meal. In the centre of the table was the bowl of mealie meal made, as the custom is, into a conical pile of the white mush smoothed over. Round it in other dishes were our sausages, corned beef and beans, warmed for us. Now we must take lumps of the mealie mush, roll it in our fingers into a ball, and with the fingertips dip it into the other dishes to sop up the contents, and so to our mouths. It is customary to do this with appreciative sucking sounds. I strove then, as I have at other times, to eat heartily of *nshima*, but hunger became faint and vanished after a very little striving. I concluded that I am just not a suitable subject for *nshima* and the more so when the mealie meal is partnered by canned sausages, corned beef and baked beans.

Our host's wife, who served us, was his junior wife, a 'coloured' and a very pretty girl, pale amber, with large pansy eyes. She might have been twenty though I think she was a year or two less. As we ate, from the next room, separated by a varnished pitch-pine wall, there came the waking whimper of a baby, and in a moment she had whisked it from there, happy for the chance to show us. Yes, she admitted, smiling in her vast and timid pride, it was her first baby. She lingered with the baby, unwilling to lose a moment's admiration for it.

The senior wife, his first wife, was a much older woman. Both wives and the husband lived under the same roof, junior wife and husband in one part and, separately, the senior wife—she entirely unresentful. This was the natural order of things.

It was later that day that, without the Professor, I went to Nangweshi. Nangweshi, they told me at Senanga, means 'tiger fish', and perhaps, they added, that is because there are many tiger fish in the river at Nangweshi and they are big ones. Where then should I go to fish for tiger fish but Nangweshi and by doing so I met James Simpson. Also, being there, I was told that Nangweshi did not mean 'tiger fish'; it meant, freely translated, 'the place where the royal spears of the chief are kept'. Never mind, it still seemed a good excuse to fish for tiger fish, and James Simpson was very pleasantly ready to take me in his boat. He was a large rufous big-boned Scotsman, a bit gruff at first from, I believe, sheer unaccustomedness to chances of sociability and conversation. He warmed to it quickly and became the affable man that, I guess, nature made him. His was an isolated life— he ranched on behalf of the government, ranching a very large

150

area of bush, largely forest, sheer jungle. And, though only partly a game reserve, it was very rich in game. I think he saw few people.

We did go on the river, going upstream and there were indeed many tiger fish which were not only as large as they were reported, but as massively ferocious as big tiger fish could be expected to be. It is by no chance and no exaggeration that they are called tiger fish.

'I use only very heavy lines for these tiger here,' James Simpson said, looking dubiously at my 12 lb breaking strain line with which, quite successfully, I had coped with tiger elsewhere; and when, about an hour later, three violently rumbustious tiger had broken the line, taking the lure and leaving me with none, I admitted his wisdom.

We went back and, walking up from the river, I stopped several times to pick up pieces of semi-precious stone.

'Aye, ye'll find plenty of that here among the stones,' James Simpson said, 'but now let's go in for some tea,' and he took me to the bungalow displaying the invincibly British addiction to afternoon tea which I, being British, found touchingly welcome in so outlandishly unexpected a setting for it. It came, authentic, true British afternoon tea—the jam and the bread and butter, with cakes after and the good strong tea poured from a teapot that could be bought in any home high street. And we were in the green-filtered shade of the verandah, the teak and the mahogany and other heavy-leafed trees stood outside and beyond the great Zambezi flowed. I could hear the coughing sighs of the hippos, and ibis settled in the trees with clattering wings.

James's wife brought the tea, fluttering a little with shyness, serving us and leaving quite soon half reluctant, half grateful, because we were so strangely unusual for her to encompass. She was African, slight and young and delightful, a dark pretty wisp. She found courage soon to bring the children to show us, the two of them, eight months and two years with charm that comes, so often, from the mixing of the two, black and white.

He talked over tea, told us of what he did there—and that was everything, farming such of the land as was under cultivation, the forestry, everything, and always with the wild disputing his charge. Every year, he said, he shot up to a dozen lion. One of them, recently, had been a man-eater; it had taken one of his men. It left just the head and the hands.

In the bar that night it was as the night before—as it was every night as I found by devoted attendance. I was, I suppose, quiet, a little apart for the time being, watching. My neighbour told me I was quiet; why was I quiet? People who have beards, he said, are people who talk a lot, so then, again, why was I quiet? Almost any question deserves answer and I explained.

'I am allowing my beard to grow too,' he told me, 'not because I want to talk a lot but because my brother died not long ago. I am Bemba you see, and it is our tribal custom to let our beards grow if a relative dies.'

The Professor did not come to the bar. Parting from us he promised that next day he would conduct us to Livingstone's tree on the other bank, the east bank, and from there down to the Sioma Falls where they may be approached from the east side. And, at seven o'clock next morning, there he was at the rest house with the driver who, newly immaculate each morning, was never twice in the same clothes, nor did the longest and most roasting day in the Land Rover seem able to produce a crumple on him.

We were ready—and that 'we' needs re-defining. Kay was not with me on this part of the journey and for that unhappy fact my solace was John Kabemba. Kay was Lozi, John was Bemba; Kay was little, a delicate dark slip, John was robust and roundly buxom, quite a broth of a man who could look forward to a weight problem. John was a *bon viveur*, happy with his beer and jolly for conversation; a rollicking man when the mood was with him.

So that was the 'we'—the Professor, John Kabemba and I— and first we went again to Sioma because it was from there we must get the ferry to take us to the east bank. But 'ferry' in this context had a special connotation. Anticipating it I thought much of the Land Rover I had seen wrecked on the rocks below the falls. There were some differences between this ferry and others, such as the one three miles or so below Senanga. That, and others on the river, were mechanically propelled. They had strong throaty engines which though often indisposed were, when working, strong. And they, all those others which I saw, worked on the more mildly undramatic reaches. But this one at Sioma had no engines. Along either side below the gunwales there was a walkway to accommodate men with poles and, on seeing them, it seemed a hardly adequate number of men. They were all the motive power. And the water they must fend against was not a gently even flow but was where the river begins to gather itself to make its huge plunge over the falls. The river was heavy with its speed of flow; it had white breaks in places. Torments on the surface gave clues to hidden shoals. But, I said to myself to build reassurance, you are not to be a pioneer; these men have made this crossing before. This is their job. So far they have returned alive. 'So far'? But it was defeatist to dwell on that phrase.

We went aboard. That is to say that the pontoon was man-oeuvred slowly and with very great care, sidling against the bullying of the current, until one end (it had no distinction of stern and stem) was nudged into the bank in a place where the Land Rover had a chance of negotiating a steep slope of sand at something like the same angle as the slope down into the pontoon. The Land Rover felt its way down, inch by inch.

Casting off, we headed largely upstream, going at about 45 degrees to the flow and, once we were steaming, I was comforted to see how confidently and competently the men contended with the river's force. Their arc was well-judged and took us finally into a gentle settlement at a landing place set in among the giant stands of *matete* reed.

There is no road on the east bank. It seemed at first as if there was nothing at all on the east bank that appertained to human-kind. At our landing point it was open, sun-blanched grass and lonely oil palms, and beyond that, downstream, heavy bush, forest. But, as we came to it, it proved not to be trackless. There was a track, not fully wide enough for the Land Rover's width, and with the grass pressed, as it seemed, almost to a polish. It went uncertainly, bending to avoid trees and denser thickets, and about it the forest was unbroken—though this was not forest of the dark and secret kind. It was largely open to the sun, going in glades and thickets, but becoming dense in areas. The effect of its vistas was the unbroken roll of it as I had seen it from the other bank, and now the recurrently seen prospects showed the shining magnificence of the river's breadth dividing a denseness of forest that lay to the horizons. It was beautiful forest, very varied in its trees and shrubs and viney growths that clambered the full height of trees, often heavy with blossom.

Now, early in the rains, it was the season for blossom—though there seems to be no season without some blossom—but the rains bring abrupt burgeoning. The ground, baked to cracking for nine months, receives the rain and immediately leaves and petals are miraculously there, almost before the watching eye. They spring from the rock-hard naked soil with such spontaneous speed, before any support of grass can come, that they sometimes have almost an artificial look, like prop flowers stuck on a naked stage. One with spiky, brilliant red blossoms, four inches across, grew everywhere in the more open places; it is called *wife of the rains*.

It was remote country, with almost an archaic remoteness—I

could see no sign that a motor vehicle before ours had passed—but evidence of human presence recurred and at last a vehicle, as archaic as the place seemed. I wondered for how many centuries its like had been there. From before the dawn of the wheel certainly, because this had none. It was a sledge, primitively made, close to the ground on heavy wooden runners, ox-drawn; it was that which gave the grass the polish I had noticed earlier. The track was a sledge way connecting settlements—they hardly justified the title of village. There were rough cultivated patches from time to time, broken from the virgin soil by ox-drawn wooden ploughs.

A party of girls came out of the bush carrying immense burdens of fruit, incongruously carried in big enamel store bowls, and their presence suggested a settlement. We came to it soon.

The forest opened and fell back. To the right lay the river, very wide, broken with islets and outcrops, surging over rocks in the quickening flow. The track ran on up a long grassy slope, past a group of enormous and ancient fig trees to huts just overtopping the rise. Children swarmed down in shouting excitement, surrounding us, running with the Land Rover. They wore only a waist cord with, front and back, a flap of material. The dogs came too, lean and rangy beasts as unused to strangers as the children, making a fierce show of standing hackles. The children laughed joyfully, the dogs snarled; the adults, coming to us when we stopped, were courteous and friendly. All the community except the very old greeted us.

'We shall come soon to Livingstone's tree,' the Professor said when we left, and when we came to another group of huts he said we should stop. The tiny village lay up from the river for immunity from the floods and we walked the hundred yards or so of grassy slope that dropped to the river.

'It was here that Livingstone walked, often, going to his tree when he wished to be alone. Soon we shall see the tree.'

We came to the bank. There was no tree. The bank lay open to either side.

'This *is* the place—but the tree—it was here, where we stand. Ah—yes—you see the hollow—that is where it grew. Perhaps, at last, it fell in a storm.'

The Professor stood, sadly wishing he could conjure for us the sense of the tree and Livingstone in its shade. He had no need to for me. Perhaps the soil had the sense of him; I felt his long-gone presence, almost tangibly. I looked at the great lonely river and thought I saw it with his eyes. It ran sibilantly, gathering its hastening weight for the coming plunge. For that moment I saw it as if I had found it after desperate months of walking from the coast.

It became wider nearer the falls. We stopped where the ground dropped in a rocky scramble; a labyrinth of channel and island went into a distance hard to estimate. I could not with certainty tell where the far bank was; it could not have been less than a mile and a half away. There was such a confusion of river and fall, broken, intersected. I guessed its whole shape could be seen only from the air—which I did confirm later, flying low over it.

A huge sill, with the shine of the river above, ran in great terraces of rock dropping down to the gorges below; in all the fissures and breaks in the terraces the myriad minor falls within the rock gave the river piecemeal descent.

I left the bank, walking the terraces, leaping the fissures, clambering as I could, guided by the distant roar of the main falls. The sound of water enclosed me, separate sounds of rills and minor cascades uniting with the growing roar to fill the air. It created an excitement, a supra-normal exhilaration; it seemed to lift the weight from the body, to make me go wing-heeled. The bank was far behind now and with it all normal world. Lodged between rocks I found a little wooden pot.

I could see it was not of these times—even remote villages have their store of enamel or aluminium pots. The wood was *muKwa*, worn and bleached by water, about four inches high. It had a simple graceful shape, forming a partial neck above the middle with a band there of simply tooled decoration. What flood of how many years ago, I wondered, had lodged it there? I learnt subsequently that it was the work of either the Toka or the Leya people, whose area is lower down the river, in the vicinity of the Victoria Falls. There—on the Kalahari Sands—there is a shortage of clay for the making of pots. So they, the Toka and the Leya, turned to the crafting of wooden pots and achieved some fame for it. One, seeing my pot, said it was for the keeping of cream. After so much immersion it still had the stain of cream in its bottom—and still the aromatic smell that *muKwa* has.

I went, at a guess, half a mile, perhaps three-quarters, across the rock terraces, then came to what, when the river is not flooding, are the main falls. I stood on an edge of rock. The boiling rush of water from the first of the falls roared through the gorge under my feet. The stones of the gorge walls were—even more than on the far bank—enormous, stacked up by the gargantuan force of floods. Now, at the river's low level, the thunderous horseshoe of the falls made rock and air tremble. Beyond the first fall there was a recession of others, from each standing its column of spume.

The others had come now, quite composed, as if the place found no string to reverberate in them. I was unwilling to lose the mood of it before I must, and headed back alone.

On the rocky slope above the river, in the chequered shade, John Kabemba made impromptu camp—in physical things he had a ready and robust sense of the practical. In an embrasure between rocks he made a hearth and in it a fire of sticks and on that, with love, began to cook.

I looked at the stones. I never saw stones more extraordinary and beautiful than those by Sioma Falls. The old volcanic fury that had built so much of Africa had brewed them up. Some had a cellular, clinkered structure which looked as if they had cooled only yesterday from the furnace. Some were crimson, banded inside with amber. Others had the yellow conglomerate of pea-like crystals such as I had found on the west bank. One stone, prised from the soil, was like a brain, crimson on its surface, inside with the look and touch of jade, yellow, not quite translucent.

John, shining hot at his fire, announced the serving of the meal. In the wilderness he had produced a quite elaborate casseroled dish, with vegetables. He served it on plates, with knives and forks. We ate well; I thought of the rough and hungry days up-river.

We returned without haste. There was a summery contentment, something nostalgic—though the sun had heat such as by-gone English summers never had. They greeted us again in the settlements, now as old friends. A kind of beatitude had settled. The same mood had fallen upon John and the Professor. They began to sing, side by side, large and little, beginning with a low chanting in the African idiom. That enlarged and swelled, John, as it seemed, leading, the Professor responding. They sang on through the forest exactly in the afternoon spirit of it, sometimes loudly together, sometimes in their duologue. I listened and dreamed of cold beer. About mid-afternoon we came to that savannah where the pontoon ferry had landed us.

It had been arranged that it should return for us about this time. It was not there. It was utterly still. The weight of heat lay on everything. I stood because being vertical gave less surface to receive the sun's pressure. I stared over the water, the cicadas shrilled, the frogs throbbed in the *matete* forests.

The pontoon came. A hundred yards out it went aground. The hot air stirred and bulged for a while with the shouting and striving to get the pontoon off. Then, that done, the air lay prone again. It was about four o'clock when we drove into Sioma.

In our party was a Boma messenger, smart in red and blue, whose native village Sioma was. His brother lived there still. We must go to his brother's house the messenger said—it was their tribal custom that a man shall not go to his brother's village without him, and those with him, being a guest to a meal in the brother's house. His brother received us hospitably, with shy courtesy, smiling as he bowed us into his house, holding back the blanket that hung to close the door. The house was built of modern materials, some sort of prefabricated sheeting, thatched with grass, but arranged inside in the common African way, with the living area divided from that for sleeping by hanging blankets. With his polite manners he waved us to low stools round the low table, then went to summon his wives. They came, an older one and a young one, and he instructed them—we were to have a complete *nshima*—and *how* was I to cope with that, two hours after the ample meal by the falls? And my thirst was now so great that I felt it could call aloud for itself.

I whispered to John. An errand of mercy did soon bring beer from the store. But, still, I cringed at the imminent *nshima*. I thought the others must be in equal distress.

It came soon, too soon. The wives, tremulously bashful, set down the mountain of *nshima* mealie mush and a matching dish of chicken. How were we, so recently replete, to honour such hospitality? I looked at the faces of the others, expecting them to be as sicklied as mine felt. They were calm. I even thought I saw anticipation.

I need have worried only for myself. The others set about the meal. Politely, they wolfed it. They rolled the mealie mush, sloshed in the chicken dish, sucked appreciatively. I mimed what I could.

We all felt better when we left Sioma. We were jolly in the Land Rover. Very early John and the Professor had settled naturally into a cross-talk act—John, ebullient, bawdy, leg-pulling, the

Professor pawkily shamming stooge. Now John, practical as always about such things, revealed that he had beer in the back. He had stocked up in Sioma. It stimulated conversation.

'Witch doctors,' declaimed the Professor, when I had made a passing reference to them. 'Witch doctors are a myth believed in by people who do not know Africa and our African ways—doctors, yes, wise men who make cures and who divine for people who have a sickness—but that is not the same.'

'Oh—ho,' John threw an ample arm over the Professor's shoulders, shaking him mildly. 'Oh-ho, you say that! No witch doctors. Is that for a joke? Always there have been plenty of witch doctors.'

The Professor raised his arms with clenched hands; he raised his voice. 'No, no, it is just something that people say—it is just superstition—that belongs to the past—we are not silly now.'

The argument rose and flared; they shouted fiercely. I became a little worried for the peace. The uproar lasted for several miles until, as we came on to the Matebele Plain, John looked out, asked as if struck by a passing thought—'Oh what's this place famous for? I've forgotten.'

The Professor paused. 'Eh? That? That's the Matebele Plain—where they used to send all the witch doctors.' He stopped, mouth dropped; he looked at John. Then both burst into roars of laughter, throwing arms round each other's shoulders. They laughed out the next mile.

We talked of missionaries too; they were united on that—with an attitude that I noticed often, half hostility, half ridicule. It was as if (or so I guessed) having largely rid themselves of the inheritance of indigenous religious beliefs, they had only caustic scepticism for an imported one. And, they were ever ready to tell you, they regarded missionaries as inseparable from colonial exploitation.

Did I, the Professor asked, know how Senanga came by its name?

*The Zambezi at
the Barotse Plain*

Sausage tree,
Barotse Plain

'It's all to do with the Boma you see—it has been moved about quite a lot since the early days, really like several experiments. Right at the beginning, when the Senanga District was first organized, the Boma was put on a mound in the flood plain, close to the Zambezi, near Nalolo, which is right away in the far northwest corner of the District.

'This did make it rather a long way for people to come from other parts of the District when they had to present their complaints to the District Commissioner—though, in those days it was not as difficult as it would be now. The floods were not as high then as now; people didn't always have to leave the plain, during the rainy season floods and so the Boma was able to get on well enough.

'But that changed. The time came when the floods became higher and, year by year, the Nalolo Boma could not be used during the floods. The seasonal system had to be used, and another flood-time Boma was set up at Muoyo. So it went Nalolo-Muoyo—Nalolo—Muoyo—season by season, and that went on right up to the end of the 1920s.

'But that was awkward, wasn't it? It's a wonder it went on so long—and then they did think it was time to have one Boma that could be used all the year and that everyone could come to quite easily. They found a place right in the middle of the District at the village of Headman Mr Senanga. They built a new Boma there, right in his courtyard. That is where it is today.

'That was, I think, 1931, and the first District Commissioner there was Mr Robinson—and you know, a D.C. then was almost like God in his district, head of just everything, administration, prison, veterinary service—and he was the judge, and the judge of appeal. On everything he was the final authority; his word was law. Of course he couldn't speak the local languages usually and he had an official interpreter. That man would be the only educated one at the Boma—he would be about the level of, say, standard IV at Senanga Secondary School of today. He would be of noble birth too.

'Yes, the D.C. was absolute ruler. He had to have people to enforce his rule, to keep law and order, and that is how the Boma messengers started. There was just one thing they were chosen for; big and strong, that's what they had to be. If a man was big and heavily built he could apply; he had to look as if he could apply force. Almost always they were illiterate.

'Then they didn't have this smart uniform they have now— no well-pressed tailored shorts and red round the blue. They wore *mulamba*. That was a cloth, rectangular, about a yard long and usually red. You wrapped it between the legs and fastened it round the loins—that word *mulamba* means loin cloth, and that is why the Boma Messengers' Compound is now called the *Mulumba Compound*. And then they didn't have the fine brick-built houses they have now; they slept in grass huts.

'The head messenger used to go with the D.C. when he went on tour—you know, collecting taxes, taking a census, checking on health, and so on. Of course there were no roads then; the D.C. was carried in a *musempula*, a sort of hammock, and men were paid at not more than a shilling a day for that. That was *not* a job you applied for—you would be selected, and that meant it was compulsory.

'The river was the only other way of travelling—that was the way to go to Livingstone. It took ten days.

'Well, it's all different now, isn't it? There are some roads now. The biggest change though was in 1934, when the airstrip was made. That brought a landing every week of a Beaver bringing supplies from Livingstone. Senanga has grown up—look at the fine secondary school we have now.'

The Professor rolled his head and absently took a pull at the fresh bottle of beer John had opened for him.

'Hm, hm, hm, yes, things have changed. We are educated and

sensible now, we've got rid of superstition and all silly things.' He looked slyly at John. 'Only ignorant people could believe in such things as spells and witch doctors.'

'And that's most people, Bwana.' John laughed, tipped his bottle, wiped his mouth. 'The witch doctors still have good business, my friend.'

The day was going. We remembered that the last ferry crossing was at six o'clock. Our driver urged the Land Rover to its maximum pace on the lumpy road. We bounded and bumped and drinking from the bottle was hazardous. It was not far from sundown when we reached the ferry; the pontoon was leaving the east bank and we must wait for it. I went apart a little because at sunrise and sunset on the Zambezi a spell falls. At evening, when the blaze has gone and the horizons are luminous, there is an unearthly peace. It is brief of course; when we had crossed the river and before we came into Senanga it was dark.

13

Muimui Nakamboa, who was a pupil of the secondary school at Senanga, wrote an essay for the school magazine. I doubt if he could have guessed its whole significance.

'The problem of today's governments is how to develop a healthy and well fed nation but very few, if any, have achieved this. The government of my country has, in order to achieve this, introduced a quantity education system. In my district there are 109 Upper Primary schools and nearly all children above 6 years go to school, three-quarters of whom continue to Secondary School level.

'Education is going to help greatly the people in my district towards better standards of health and food. The standard of living in my district is at present very low. The people still live in windowless, dark huts which are usually surrounded by tall grasses. They still keep on living in the marshy plains, the home of the mosquitoes. With ignorance blinding my people they do not have rubbish pits. They do not have lavatories thus usually in the bushes surrounding the villages live hook-worm and many other germs. The flies carry the germs to the dirty food the people eat.

'With education opening the minds of the people in my district these conditions will change. The children who go to school are taught how to prevent germs from attacking people by living in clean conditions. They are told to dig lavatories rather than use the bush. They are taught to dig rubbish pits and throw the waste materials in the pits rather than scatter them about their homes. When these children come home they tell their parents this thing and encourage them to do the same things. The children explain to them the badness of flies, mosquitoes and hookworm from the waste matters. They explain to them why they should live in clean surroundings. They tell them that when they cough at night it is not because there are spirits in the house but because there is not enough air for them to breathe. With this knowledge the people will gradually change and the standard of health will be greatly improved.

'The education development helps my people towards better standards of food. The village people usually keep their cooked foods open. The food which has gone bad to them is the best. For example my grandfather would prefer a two-day-old fish which has gone bad to a fresh fish just out of the river. My people prefer sour milk to fresh milk to drink.

'Such ignorance can only be overcome by education—by teaching and showing the young generation the badness of these things and by showing them better methods of cooking and preserving their food materials.

'As education started a few years ago some of its results have been seen in some villages situated near schools and bomas. The people begin to build big houses with windows. They sell their milk while still fresh and live in considerably cleaner homes. The wells and places where drinking water is got are kept safe from animals and children. Really education is helping a lot the people in my district towards better standards of health and food. Thanks to it!'

So short a time ago Senanga was a tiny village of grass huts nowhere in particular in the roadless enormity of the Plain. Now its secondary school has 600 pupils, and Muimui Nakamboa is one of them. What he has learnt at Senanga other children are learning in other secondary schools all over Zambia.

165

Sope Mulemwa, in the same magazine, comments that a majority of the ideas brought from Europe to Africa have become an integral part of African convention—the daily washing of the face, eating from plates. 'Our ancestors,' he says, 'had no notion of these conventions nor could they even foresee them.' Sometimes, he adds, students complain—'Why do these Europeans compel us to use forks and knives even when eating *nshima?*'

He has thoughts about other things. He is sedate.

' "What makes life beautiful and pleasant?" I have often asked my colleagues. Their response to this question has always been that a pleasant life can only be attainable if one gets married to a very beautiful woman. Unfortunately, I hold a different opinion.

'I do not mean to criticize them, but to let them envisage what is lying in wait for them. Before one gets married, he must remember that, as an exceptionally bright flower in the middle of a plain attracts more insects, so will a very beautiful wife magnetize many men. A woman whose beauty is current gossip to all who happen to see her is not good for a wife. Beauty on its own can never make life pleasant, but the disposition of the couple towards each other is what really matters.

'So, take warning, my friends: Mark Antony lost not only an Empire but also his life because of an Egyptian Beauty—Queen—Cleopatra!'

Perhaps scepticism about women starts early among the boys of Senanga. Likando Moyawonyambe had reached only class IIIA and was, I suppose, not a very big boy, but already firm about women.

'All women long most to control their husbands and lovers!

'All women like to be thought of as being sensible while others are not!

'They like luxury and delicacies while they can't afford to buy them!

'They like to possess everything.

'They like to be honoured.

'They all like amusements.

'They like to be married often by different men!'

Three young voices, probably as representative as any three could be. They convey the curious amalgam of old and new attitudes. Cheek by jowl with Muimui Nakamboa's eager grasping of the future, Katunda Nawa gives an illustrated piece on how to make kachipembe—as if, in a school magazine in, say, Sutton, Surrey, there were a piece on the making of potato whiskey. But he is admonitory.

'People buy this spirit at fifty *ngwee* per bottle and five people can share one bottle among themselves.

'I advise you not to take this kind of drink because it is not good for HEALTH.'

Saponeka Nyambe, of IIA, quite a small boy presumably, had a dream which, as he wrote it, has a beauty. He called it, *How I came to Know the Position of my Heart*.

'It was not long after daylight when I realized that I was among gigantic trees. I sat miserable over a piece of wood. At that moment I was like a mite and soon I heard a mob towards the northeast of my position. I did not know what caused me to go there. On my way I had to stop and when I looked to the side I caught a glimpse of a ghost. I said to myself: "This is a dreadful thing to appear to a person like me!" I heard as if someone was saying to me, "Look down." Soon after I raised my head the ghost had disappeared. I sat on the ground leaning against a big curved rock.

'It took me a long time before I gained strength. I felt a gentle wind, so I raised my head and saw a bird as if dancing for welcoming a guest. I saw that its wings were as long as a man's arms. Its neck was long and I saw something coiled on it. So I picked up a stone and threw at it and hit on the neck. The bird almost fell to the ground but there fell a snake from its neck which was coiled round it. The bird flew away freely. I did not trouble myself to go and see what kind of snake it was because I was powerless. I felt very hot and sat upon my knees.

'For a long time, I listened very attentively because I heard as if someone was beating a piece of metal against something. I was very frightened till I came to know it was something in my body. I touched every place in search of the position of the beating noise. After a while, I found that it was inside between the chest and the back of my body—on the left-hand side!'

The final balance of Europe's impact on Africa is hard to assess. Seen through the eager eyes of Muimui Nakamboa it seems upliftingly beneficent—ignorance, disease, superstition, falling back before the flaming sword of education, and, so far, that is true. If it were all the truth the western world must be almost an earthly paradise. But a note in passing in the school's horticultural survey is innocently sinister. For insects, it says, insects such as grasshoppers and beetles and cutworms, which have been found to be attacking plants, senior staff and the Y.F.C. sprayed with D.D.T. European culture comes two-handed, bearing honeyed enlightenment with one and lethal contamination with the other. The threat is dire that white hands will have lifted Africa from primitiveness to social and environmental decline with hardly a pause in the intervening stage of a benign and wholesome civilization—though, looking back, it is hard to see a point at which Europe's own long climb from savagery had quite positively settled at such a blessed state. It is irresistible to think that it may prove to be that the West has hustled Africa out of its original ignorance and disease into something, in the end, far more deadly.

'It is important that no one shall be ignorant,' the Professor said as we drove out of Senanga in the early sun. 'When everyone is educated it will be a good world.' But he, who had a loving care for all that had made the past and for every aromatic thread and fibre of the lore of his people, would have been appalled if a prophetic vision could have shown him the Barotse Plain brought to the state of much of the industrial West.

Now, as we went in the Land Rover, he was in a state of happy obsession. We were going to *Lambwata*, the place of the tomb, and he could not contain the ripe knowledge that bubbled in him. We left the slight rise that held Senanga above the plain and passed again into the emptiness where the hugeness of the sky seemed to press the land flat.

'*Lambwata* is on a mound—you will see—and that's where the regal tomb is, in the charge of *Anamwi*—he is the priest of the tomb.'

'But whose tomb was it?'

'That of Mwanambinyi—he was Litunga, but a long time ago —three hundred years ago. It was there, on his burial mound that he went into the ground.'

'Went into the ground? He was buried there?'

'No, not that really. He was still full of living and the power of his authority, but, because all must come to death and burial at some time, he preferred to choose his own time of going. He would go into the ground of his own volition. There, with all his people and all his cattle and his indunas—his counsellers you know —he sank into the ground. They preferred to go with him. And there they are now, he and they, still alive.'

'Alive?'

'Oh yes—you see he would not submit just to waiting till he died; he went down in his life and his life continues.'

The Professor stopped, paused. 'Well,' he said, 'that is the old story—just superstition of course.'

'Was this,' I asked, 'the same Litunga who ruled at Mongu?'

'Ah no—there were always two Litungas, the one who ruled in the Mongu area and the other here in the south, and neither had authority over the other. This one, Mwanambinyi, was the son of Mboyu—she was the daughter of Mwambwa who was married to a spirit—and, that same spirit married the daughter of Mboyu.'

The Professor looked at me, pausing I think so that I should have at least some chance of absorbing what poured from him—and there was so much and it gushed so quickly that I have no confidence that I have it accurately. He did correct me as to the sinking into the ground of Mwanambinyi and his people—I had misheard him, he said, it was only the indunas who sank with their master, not the people and the cattle too. But did I know about the making of the Litunga?

'You must understand that the Litunga is the son of God— "Litunga" means king—he is far more deeply respected than even the greatest chief because he is elected by the cow spirit. That is *Lyombekalala*, the sacred cow which has no beginning and no end. It comes out of the river and, to everyone but the Litunga it is invisible—only the Litunga can see it. The sacred cow licks the new Litunga all over and that is a sign that he is accepted by God. Then the people give the new Litunga his mounds—they give him three, three of these man-made mounds that stand above the floods. He has one for a dry season residence, one for a rainy season residence, and one for burial.'

'But now you will understand why this place, Lambwata, is so sacred. Not only, you see, did the Litunga Mwanambinyi sink into the ground there, but he is there still, alive, in the ground. To all Lozi people it is very holy and all who come to it, all Lozi people, kneel there and chant out loud "Yo-sho—Yo-sho" and as they do that they bend their head to the ground and up again and then down again. They repeat "Yo-sho—Yo-sho" several times. But now, look—there is the place, we are coming to it.'

We were passing the scattered herds of cattle, lean wide-horned beasts that looked as if there was little of milk or meat they could give but, it could be guessed, of desperate importance to the tiny community on the mound ahead. It had grown from a kinking of the horizon and was now definable with huts and a few great old leaning trees. We came near to it and the children and dogs swarmed out to meet us, coming to us and running with us.

We stopped and, getting out, were encompassed not only by the whole population—men, old women, suckling mothers, the medley of children and dogs—but as much by the almost overwhelming immensity of isolation. The dusty hubbub of the people enhanced rather than lessened the sense of the pressure of space beyond—the whole place, the whole human enclosure, could not have been more than an acre—and beyond that, pressing on every side, the enormous nothingness. The human uproar was absorbed and lost almost before it had crossed the mound's perimeter. One tree, bare-stemmed, very tall, had its crown entirely filled by a host of snake birds—which, presumably, would not have been there if the place did not give them a good living. There were other trees, majestically gnarled, nearly bare from their huge bifurcating boles to the leathery mass of their crowns.

'Yes,' the Professor said. 'They are great trees. They come from the time of Mwanambinyi.'

Among the people was the priest, *Anamwi*, lean and nervous. Could he, we asked, perform the act of reverence and, though he led us to the edge of the unmarked circle, he would go no further. It was grass, and we knew its shape because the people stood by but would not cross its circumference. At the circle's centre stood a tree.

'No, it was not planted to mark the place, it just grew there, just by chance,' the Professor said. 'But it does exactly mark the place where Mwanambinyi sank.'

It was the custom, they told us, to make a gift before the act of reverence would be performed, if someone wanted to watch; I gave the priest seventy-five *ngwee*. It was not enough, he said, and, when we gave him more, still protested. But it became plain that it was not greed but fear—he would have asked more and

171

more as a device to avoid entering the circle. His protesting hands trembled; he shrank back against those behind him.

The act was performed. A young man came forward wearing an easy air of no-nonsense non-belief. He would do it, do it for nothing, and so he did, though with a slight manner of bravado. The others laughed uneasily, making rather ample room for him as he left the circle.

When we left the tiny village on its mound the passing from it was abrupt. To its last foot the friendly noise of it was loud. Then, in a moment, we had gone into the bottomless silence of the plain and the people were miming figurines, waving soundlessly as if seen through a window.

The plain was silent but the Professor was not. From the back of the Land Rover his flood of learning poured on, hard to follow with his soft and rapid speech matched against the noise of the engine. I never did hear the end of his story about a Litunga of three hundred years ago, nor did I learn if it was this same Mwanambinyi. The people of Sesheke, well to the south and on the last edge of Lozi territory, had revolted against the Litunga, seeking freedom. The Litunga came vengefully with an expedition to quell the rebels and, on his way, came to the village of Malombe which, though young then, is one of the oldest villages in the Barotse country. In the village dwelt a man who, for a reason the Professor's story did not explain, disliked the Litunga and, in the night, secretly crossed the river to where the Litunga was encamped. With intent to do death to the Litunga he shot an arrow, which, missing the Litunga, hit a drum. It was a very particular drum, and though, as I think, the Professor did not tell me the reason of it, it had to be played for so many hours every day. So, the Professor said, the drum was silenced and the Litunga was not and, at this point, the Professor became portentous, sinking his voice meaningfully but, for the hearing of the story, fatally. Curiosity as to the end of that story has continued maddeningly.

172

Probably, and the Professor suggested it, the would-be assassin of the Litunga was of another tribe. Misunderstandings of many kinds may arise between tribes, and for no reason more than language differences which while not having difference enough to prevent communication can lead to devious misunderstanding.

'Yes, oh yes,' John said, 'there was a soldier, a Ngoni—the Ngoni are from right the other side of Zambia near the Mozambique border—who, being posted to Western Province, was on patrol in the bush for three weeks, seeing few people apart from other soldiers. Certainly he had seen no girls. Then with some others he was given off duty and went to one of the Boma villages in Western Province. He met a girl there, a nice Lozi girl, nicely shaped. He spoke to her in his Ngoni language.'

I cannot swear to the accuracy, as John told us, of what he said, but it was, I think, *'Ine mukazi nikufuma'*. But as to its meaning in English, that was succinct—'You girl I want you.'

'But this girl,' John went on, 'she did not speak *Ngoni*; she did not understand. "Please speak in *Sikololo*" she said, and that made the soldier very excited. He grabbed the girl by the arm— "Yes," he said, "yes, that's what I want, *chigololo*", and well, you can guess what *chigololo* means in *Ngoni*. The girl screamed. "Don't scream, don't scream," the soldier said to her, grabbing her more tightly, "you've pronounced it already."

'Just then an officer was passing; he asked the girl what was happening. "This man is dragging me, and I don't know why." The man saluted—"It's all right, she has said it, what I want, *chigololo*. She's just said it."

'The officer explained, and the girl said, "Ohhh", and started laughing. "All right then? You understand each other now?" the officer said, and then he left them.'

'And what then?' I asked John.

'Well—they did understand each other now, didn't they?'

14

The District Governor and the District Secretary saw us off when we left Senanga, and I see them still, tall and tiny, warm and admirable men. There was a melancholy in the parting.

Our next objective was Katima Mulilo on the west bank and Sesheke on the other—not, as might seem, the east bank but the north. To Katima Mulilo the river runs south-west but there it turns abruptly to run almost due east, thus making Sesheke, a few miles downstream, on the north bank. Nor is that the only change. To Katima Mulilo the river is wholly Zambian, with Western Province on both banks. But there it becomes a frontier. On the north bank it is Zambia, on the south bank it is South-West Africa, at that oddity of political geography which is known as the Caprivi Strip—a narrow corridor of land debouching from the main body of South-West Africa to prise between Zambia and Botswana (which used to be Bechuanaland).

For the hundred and ten miles from Nangweshi to Katima Mulilo the river runs with splendour. The falls at Sioma are the consummate apex of that, but for all the distance the majesty of its breadth is a succession of rapids coming often to boiling cataracts, and, by the confluence with the Lumbe River, there was said to be a monster in the river.

It lived in a whirlpool, waiting there till men came in their canoes. Then it would seize them, devouring man and canoe. So the story went, and undoubtedly many men had been snatched there, never to be seen again. And, also without doubt, there was a monster there, though it was the power of the river itself and no awful reptilian creature. So great is the suctional force of the whirlpool that, as a fisheries biologist who was researching the river told me, he would not risk taking his very fast and powerful boat upon it. 'And,' he added, 'it's such a queer and depressing place that I wouldn't find it difficult to believe in a malignant monster there.'

I was not long at Katima Mulilo and, while there, stayed at the rest house which is set up the slope from the river, just above the berthing place of the pontoon ferry. By the ferry I commuted often to Sesheke, going at first light sometimes and sometimes a little later when the children crossed too, going to the school in Sesheke. Sometimes my friend the fisheries biologist would come across for me, coming in his Land Rover. As became him as a scientist, he was a soberly factual man, recording and stating what, indubitably, he saw. One morning, in the cool and early light before sunrise, we sat, he and I, in the Land Rover waiting for the coming of the ferry from the other bank. He leaned on the steering wheel, staring at the river.

'Funny thing,' he said, ruminatingly, 'the river here used to be utterly infested with croc—people were really bothered about them. The women coming for water or to wash clothes were being taken by the bloody croc, much too often.

'It got so bad they had to do something. Decided to call in the witch doctor—a specialist y'know—the croc doctor. Well, he came and he made his medicine. And, d'you know, funny thing that was, those croc went. For a hundred yards out from this bank, and for a hundred yards upstream and downstream, they never saw another croc. As thick as ever though beyond that.'

It was pleasant, in the first sun of morning, going up through the soft deep dust of the road from the ferry into Sesheke. The children were going then because those of Katima Mulilo attended school in Sesheke and in their colours they were a delicious sight.

They had uniforms according, I suppose, to age, division of school, or some such thing, and the colours of them were pure and brilliant. Some were clear bright blue, cobalt, some shining apple green, and some orange or magenta, making singing little clots of colour up the road and looking so beautifully well with the tender purple-black of their skins with a bloom upon them like black grapes. This was at the time approaching Independence Day which comes in October and is a day of great and joyous celebration over all the country. The children had their parts to play and, each morning and again at the evening crossing back, there was much practising on little drums and with pipes and singing. I was not, regretfully, present to see the celebrations because I was that day up the river catching tiger fish at the foot of the rapids. But, back in Sesheke towards evening, after all was done—ceremonies, races, football match, the dancing and the singing and all else—a lightly festal air still hung over the place though not, as I saw looking at many citizens, with the sober clarity of the morning. I think it was ending as a jolly roistering evening.

It was a heartening and luxurious change, on occasional mornings, to have breakfast at the fisheries research camp at Sesheke, in camp chairs above the river, with the hardly believable delight of freshly cooked bacon and eggs. Philosophical acceptance of the evening's baked beans and canned sausages at the rest house by the light of a paraffin pressure lamp was the more possible for that. We took them leisurely, those breakfasts, yarning for a while, feeling languidly privileged.

'There used to be a D.C. over there,' the biologist said, nodding across the river, 'who made himself about the best privy up and down the river. A big baobab tree was near his place, a hollow one. He fixed it up in there—dug it out you know, fixed up a seat. He used to love to sit there, one of his steady pleasures. Fine view over the river.'

It was as we waited one morning, bathing in the drifting scent of the cooking eggs and bacon, that they came carrying a white enamel bowl as if it held nitro-glycerine. One man carried it and others walked with him nervously cautious. There was a creature in the bowl, not much of a creature, three inches perhaps, with many legs and an inconspicuous look.

'Centipede,' the biologist said. 'Deadly little bastard. For God's sake don't get too near it.'

It did not look as lethal as that, though not an engaging animal, and not nearly as alarming looking as a scorpion which is, in fact, not normally lethal at all. You see those, the scorpions, best at night, taking out a torch. There are so many things which crawl or creep or fly in Africa and the most fearsome looking are not always the ones most to be feared. First sight of the chongololo would probably scare any newcomer.

It is, for its sort of creature, big. Really it looks rather monstrous, so obesely round, so multiple-legged, about four inches of dimly shining thing with a surface like rubbed lead. It is also excessively inactive, so creepily lethargic that that promotes distrust. But there is no need for worry even if you find yourself with chongololos to every side, as quite often you may, because they abound. They are utterly harmless, as fat and, apparently, as pointlessly stupid and chumpishly sluggish as their name suggests. Everything in nature has a purpose and so, presumably, has the chongololo. It is not an obvious one. What is most to be noticed about it is its being found dead but intact very often and without visible reason.

The chameleon has a purpose easy to see. It eats insects. But, so odd a creature is it, with such queer ways, that demonstrably harmless and helpful as it is, it is feared. But this is an animal that will in minutes, before your watching eyes, change its colour drastically, becoming dull or bright, green or pink or whatever will match its context and, waiting for victims, roll its very protuberant eyes independently in a very uncanny manner. So the people believe their instincts more than any obvious facts and they greatly fear the chameleon. It does, they say, give harbourage for the spirits of ancestors, and they may often be malignant.

I left Sesheke and Katima Mulilo and going downstream, with Zambia on the north bank and the low malarial marshes of the Caprivi Strip on the south bank, came to Kazungula. It is a frontier post, but more multiply so than most. There, they used to say, five countries meet, and though now the number is four, it is still a place to stand to count frontiers. As it used to be Northern Rhodesia, Barotseland, South West Africa, Bechuanaland and Southern Rhodesia touched frontiers there. Northern Rhodesia has become Zambia and Barotseland is now its Western Province; Bechuanaland is Botswana and Southern Rhodesia is Rhodesia, but all the four of them meet at Kazungula.

The Chobe River comes into the Zambezi there too, coming up from the south as the frontier between Botswana and South West Africa and, at the confluence, looking almost as big a river as the Zambezi. It has a significance beyond what could be guessed from acquaintance as casual as that or indeed could be guessed from a journey such as mine from that far source against the Congo— the indubitable source that is for all normal purposes and is so accepted. But, just now and then there is another and in a sense ultimate source. Its rather unlikely means is the Chobe which, upstream of its confluence with the Zambezi, is not a great river. But it is the vessel by which water coming from the Okavango River becomes, transitorily, part of a hugely enhanced Zambezi course. The Okavango rises two hundred miles from the west coast and ends with an inland delta part of which feeds Lake Ngami, but which, ordinarily, has no connection with the Zambezi. But at floodtime on the Okavango its water spills over into what is at other times a dry riverbed, the Makwegama, or, as it is called, the Makwegama Spillway and that conveys it into the Chobe and so into the Zambezi. Thus this flow which starts so near the west coast finally runs out on the east coast into the Indian Ocean.

The Chobe River has another curiosity at its point of flowing into the Zambezi—sometimes it flows backwards there, away from its parent river. The cause is an earlier flooding of the Zambezi than the Chobe, causing the former to be a few feet higher than the latter at their junction.

At Kazungula, and at Mambova a few miles upstream, I was much about the river with Joe Susman. Joe, who is white, African born and bred, and as African as anyone could be, of whatever colour. He reminded me at times of the Professor.

'There was a time,' he told me, 'when I had a job to do for my father, and I was quite young then, quite a kid I suppose, in my twenties you know. I had to bring some cattle from Maun down in Bechuanaland, as it was then, up to Kazungula. I had some herdsmen—must have been about fourteen or fifteen of us altogether. There was one night we made camp and, in the usual way, made a bush kraal—felled some trees and scrubby stuff to make a rough enclosure for the beasts and the men. But this time the lions became very troublesome during the night, rampaging round, and, in the end, breaking in. Well, they killed some of the cattle and stampeded the rest. It was a disaster you know—but there was nothing we could do till morning.

'Dawn came and we found there were sixty head of cattle missing. We had to find them, so I took my horse and rifle and three men and set out to find them. We became lost, utterly lost, and we stayed lost for five days—without water and without food. We might have died but for my rifle—I did find a bit of game and when I shot something we opened it up before anything else to find the bladder. We let the horse drink first because it was the most important and then we drank ourselves and ate the flesh raw.

'Of course we weren't doing too well on this and I don't know how long we could have gone on. But on the sixth day we met a party of bushmen, a few little men and their women, about sixteen or so. They were kind; they were good people. They took charge of us, found what had happened to us, where we had to go, all that. But, above all, they had water and, can't you imagine, we were ravenous after that. We'd have just gulped down the lot if they'd let us. When we rushed at the water they pulled us off—these little men they pulled us off with no nonsense, pulled me off. You might kill yourselves they told us, and made us drink through straws. They were right of course—but d'you know what it's like when you're really thirsty?

'They took us back to our camp and, after all we'd suffered, it turned out to be only twelve or thirteen miles away. I suppose we'd been round and round.

'It was down there too, about that country, that I used to see a lot of Frank and Archie Balm. Great hunters they were, brothers, and you couldn't have said which was the better of them when it came to stalking. They had a bet once, I remember. One of them —I think it was Frank—bet Archie that he couldn't stick a stamp on an elephant's backside and get away.

'Well, you know what elephant are like—you'd think they had ears and eyes in their backsides—and pretty nasty they'd get if they found you creeping up on them. But Archie wasn't the man to turn down a dare like that. I didn't see him do it. Wish I had. But when they found some elephant he picked out a nice big bull. He started to stalk it from about a couple of hundred yards, and I reckon his heart was in his mouth for the last fifty of that, however much faith he had in himself—if he'd cracked one small stick it could have been enough. You know what a bull elephant is like when it's with the herd.

'But he did it. Frank saw him reach up out of the grass. He got the stamp on all right—perhaps the elephant thought it was the touch of a fly—then he slid back and got away.'

For anyone who has seen much of elephant that was a story to produce a sympathy of gooseflesh. The elephant is a touchy beast which, unlike a majority of others, will not avoid confrontation if it can. It *is* an ultimate lord of its world, too big, too strong, to have effective enemies and very conscious of that. Merely to be there, however inoffensively, is enough to upset its tetchy sense of territory, and it is cautionary to know the signs of its mood. If it lifts its head and brings out and a little forward the mighty spread of its ears—an arrogant sight—it is time to leave unobtrusively. If it leans slightly backwards and lifts one forefoot it may be too late to leave. If you have the security of a vehicle that can outspeed its anger you can afford to admire the imperious splendour of it—and the African elephant is beautiful and magnificent and supremely so in its anger. Even its voice, so high and thin for so great a creature, is splendidly and wildly imperious.

Once, by Lake Tanganyika, I saw the meeting of two bull elephant in dispute over territory and cow elephant. There was a resident herd there, several cows, some calves and stripling bulls, and a bull rather past the best of his prime. It was a peaceful community. Into it there came one day a young bull from outside, hugely strong. The old bull, as he must, challenged the newcomer, going out to intercept him. They bore down upon each other in frontal assault, bringing together the battering impact of their heads and entwining their tusks. So locked they swayed in a slow thunder of trampling and striving that seemed, as it so often does in such combats of wild creatures, partly a ritual. When they did break apart after possibly ten minutes of fighting the old resident bull was, so to speak, formally defeated. He was defeated and, I suppose, deposed, but with no great injury. He had superficial bleeding cuts and abrasions but with none of the harm that it may be guessed could be the potential outcome of fighting between animals of that size.

We went fishing in the vicinity of Mambova, Joe and I and

John Castle from Livingstone, catching tiger and the great, if not very beautiful, catfish of various kinds. We also caught the several kinds of so-called largemouth and smallmouth bream, not very great but certainly extremely beautiful. Bream they are called though they do not in the least belong either to the breams of salt water or the breams of fresh water, which are themselves entirely unrelated anyway. These African breams, common in their quite numerous species in the rivers of central and southern Africa— and indeed with relatives in the waters of other parts of tropical Africa—these breams are cichlids, members of the great *Cichlidae* family that occurs widely in South America too and always with their own very particular beauty. They have a collective tendency to a pretty fancifulness, invariably with large spots over the fins, often orange or pink, and with all sorts of delicately bright bandings and flushings of colour over their banner-like fins. The most impressive, the biggest and most lushly coloured, has many names but its commonest African name, *nembwe*, suits it as well as any. That conveys, or so it seems to me, some sense of the fine fat contours of the fish, its robust butteriness of shape and colour. White African anglers commonly call it, among other things, yellow belly and it has a resplendently rounded belly of richest yellow, and all over it is pricked with gleams of gold over its general green. Some cichlids hatch their eggs in their mouths and give nursery care there after the hatching.

The extent of our fishing, and its freedom from care, was limited. The boat, normally fast and powerful, was ailing. As first warnings came of a storm, it became more obviously insecure. Then I hooked a fish, the biggest and most obdurate of the day. Probably it was a big catfish, about forty or fifty pounds, and I with the lightest sort of rod and a line of six pounds breaking strain. Such situations may be resolved finally in the fisherman's favour by an hour or two of very careful playing. But it was towards evening now, the sun was lost in the lowering of the storm's approach. Sinister small puffs of air stirred the heavy stillness. I could feel a lack of patience in Joe and John. The wide Zambezi is a poor place to be caught in darkness and the awful fury of such storms as that place has. I held the fish hard. The line broke.

No word was said. Had there been comment I think it would not have been of gratitude but—'and about time too'. We set off for Mambova. It was to be guessed which would be there first, the storm or us.

It was a dead heat. As our bow touched bank the sagging sky burst. The solid rain, the lightning, and the roar, dropped out. Scrambling, crouching under the fury, we gathered up our gear into the shelter of a petrol store by the landing place. I felt the sudden fall of temperature and began to shiver. Can it fall *so* cold in the tropics, I said to myself, and looked at my pocket thermometer. Eighty-three it read.

We were able to send a messenger willing to face the storm to bring us aid and we waited isolated in the wall of rain and its uproar on the iron roof.

'You never know quite what may happen to you, fishing on this river,' Joe said. 'There was the time we went fishing upstream of Livingstone, Sandy Innes and me.

'As you know, on the sort of water there is there, with quite a lot of rapids, you can shoot the rapids—you can go up them with full throttle, climb them, then coming back downstream you shoot them. There was one we had to come down, quite an innocent-looking one, about ten feet wide between two upstanding rocks—and our boat wasn't big, only about a ten-footer.

'Well, we went down all right, and then, just below, there was what we had never seen there before, about twenty or thirty yards down, a most ferocious whirlpool. Nothing we could do—just shot into it.

'Over we went, the boat and us. Everything in the boat—all

183

the tackle, years' collection, valuable cameras—all went. So did we. Sucked down. Force of the water was tremendous.

'I remember surfacing and, just after, so did Sandy Innes. I remember saying "You all right, Sandy?" He just had time to say "Yes" and I went down, sucked down and down and down in that vortex. I don't know how far—didn't touch bottom.

'Then I surfaced again and there was Sandy—"You all right, Joe?" he said and then, "Look, Joe—here comes the petrol can—grab it." I did grab it and, being a powerful swimmer, I was able to reach the bank—somehow or other Sandy managed to reach it too, though I didn't know that till later—just then I thought he'd gone, because he'd vanished after calling to me. Such had been the force of that water that it had stripped me, whipped off everything—lace-up shoes, stockings, shorts, shirts, underpants— just left me my wristwatch, but taken my glasses and I can't see a thing without those.

'Must have been a couple of hours after when Sandy and I found each other—both thought the other had gone—and then I saw that Sandy had an enormous gash—from his hair, down the middle of his forehead, down to the tip of his nose. Sandy found the boat too—we righted it and baled it out and found it would still float. All we could do was to work our way down-stream to an island where we might find someone we knew who lived there.

'And sure enough, when we got there and shouted this man did hear us and came out in his boat. He led us ashore and, just as we got ashore, in the state we were in, who should come down out of the trees but two gorgeous girls, friends of this chap. But they were all right, practical and helpful—threw us some towels.'

We waited about an hour and a half in the petrol store and then, when the rain stopped and the lightning died away, a police-man came down with a car to pick us up. We had to sleep some-where. Our trip had been intended as a circular one—first to

Kazungula and Mambova for a day's fishing, then on to Mulobezi among the teak forests for the night, then back to Livingstone, a three days' trip. There was a store in the village, one of those Susman's stores so often to be seen in villages—founded by Joe's family. The policeman took us there, and that, for the night, was home.'

We had a spirit stove, the store's stock provided, inevitably baked beans and stewed steak and there was canned beer. Candles provided light till we got the Tilly lamp going and then it was a sort of luxury. Mattresses from stock softened the concrete firmness of the floor and we settled to relatively peaceful sleep that was only from time to time disturbed by rats. In the morning the counters provided a place for the physical jerks needed after that night to get the reluctant blood stirring for the day.

But stir it did and I wandered down to the river to browse and watch and enjoy the air freshened by the overnight storm. The children were there too, frolicking. The girls swam in their flimsy little dresses, the boys wore nothing, like shining eels, supply slipping in the water, cavorting between the dense beds of blue-flowered water lilies. But when the boys came out of the water shame touched them because I was there. They put their hands over their genitals. They had been got at.

When they had gone and silence filled their place a woman came bringing her small son. He was, I guessed, three or four, and this was the time for his bath. As the custom is, she took him into a bay of shallow water, the naked little boy, and soaped him. Over his woolly head, over all his black and dimpled small body he was copiously sudded. He sobbed and roared very piteously, but, inexorably, cleanliness was imposed to the end.

When they had gone there was nothing again for a time but the silence and insects' hum over it till a distant jolly noise grew and came near and became a lorry bursting-full of young men in football clothes. It drew up above the river and out jumped the

185

young men. They laughed, joked, were abundant with high spirits and were immensely likeable. We talked they and I, and everything was full of their frolicsome bonhomie. We all shook hands before they climbed back into the lorry and left us lightly jolly as they had come.

'Who are they?' I asked the guard of the petrol store who had come wandering over.

'Convicts; there's a prison camp not far away.'

It was later that day I was watching a group of hippos, and they reminded me of the children bathing. They had the same bliss of water. The colour was similar too, that sepia darkness, pink-lined. The hippos were pink in the folds of their necks, pink round their eyes, pink in their ears, a pucy pink; their texture looked like velvet-satin, soft-looking—belying the sometimes ferocious behaviour of the beasts.

15

David Livingstone discovered the Falls. No white man's eye before his saw that stupendous sight. The Africans told him that the name of it was *Musi-o-Tunya*—'The Smoke that Thunders'—and that name is not only poetic but accurate. To see the great sight now as Livingstone saw it you must strive with your imagination—now you come the ten miles from the town of Livingstone on a good modern road to the Victoria Falls. How *are* you to see with the eyes of a man who, through the months of marching, with malaria and dysentery, has heard vague but persistent stories of the great smoke that thunders and which may be seen for many miles across the scorched yellow of the bush and, at last, with no real preknowledge comes to so enormous a revelation? How can you make of yourself such a man? Now the Falls are flood-lit at night.

But for all that you may still in minutes drop out of the tourism by the Falls into something like the original jungle that Livingstone saw—and even on that fine modern road it may happen, as it did to one man, that you round a bend too late to avoid a hippo crossing with her calf. That man was killed. The hippo walked on.

A track leaves the curio sellers and the modern hotel and goes down into wilderness. The jungly scarp falls into the gorge below the Falls and the track twists and clings through it. It looks little trodden, which would be hard to believe were it not invariably so. Tourism treads conformingly.

Almost at once I lost not only sight but sound too of the world above. Only yards from the cameras I had sunk into what, although overshadowed by the muffled roar of the Falls, seems to be in the wild a sort of silence—the medley of half-heard sounds which collectively makes a hush. Insects hum, birds stir and call, but the effect is deep quiet. When a bird called suddenly and loudly very close I was startled and halted. It was above my head, green, and I think it was abusing me in its odd gruff voice. It rocked on its bough, nagging. But I suppose it was frightened; it flew away showing the crimson of its flight feathers and a metallic flash of blue-green back. I was happy to be able to recognize it— it was a knysna lourie, quite large and long-tailed, a very beautifully handsome bird with a high nod of green crest that enhanced its nagging.

It was flat dry plateau above but in the precipitous privacy of this cleft spray never ceases to fall and makes a different climate and a different growth. The gorge's sheer wall traps the heat, and in that and the spray palms luxuriate, not the lank vegetable ivory ones of the savannah above but glaucous ones, green and lushly pendant. The thicket under them looked like leopard cover and, for all I knew, there could have been leopards by every bend. Their commonest prey was there—I turned a bend of track and there was a crowd of baboons, high stilt legs and bristling hackles, with the frowning yellow glare of their kind.

I stopped and they stopped, then very slowly I moved forward trying to photograph them and they, I will swear, were camera-conscious. They stayed, bottoms towards me, heads screwed round, suspicious but interested. They were nervous but wanted to stay. When I came closer they edged away with short warning grunts and showing teeth then, reluctantly, went. I was disappointed, but round the next bend through the rampant luxuriance there were two monkeys, and I had been told of their kind— 'Ferocious beasts,' someone had said, 'tear you to bits in two minutes.' Perhaps so; but not that time. They eyed me enigmatically. When I eased towards them, camera ready, they sprang away.

The track ended above a tumble of rocks, a thirty-foot drop of huge igneous slabs to the swirl below. Here was the bottom of the gorge, an awesome place, well named at this point the Boiling Pot. Just downstream, dizzily over the gorge as if a spider had thrown it across, was the bridge connecting Zambia and Rhodesia. Could it *really* carry traffic, that tenuous span? Upstream the gorge came narrowly from the face of the Falls, penning the constricted rage of the entire flow of the mile and a quarter of the river's width that drops over the Falls. It came with an appalling boiling pour in the rocky gut, and, you would think, nothing could withstand it. The sun shone and the flowers grew but there was the sense of a nether place under those three hundred and fifty lowering feet of basalt. This was still the dry season's flow. Could even *those* walls contain the full flood's force?

In a sense of course they do not, in the long term; the Boiling Pot is part of the proof of that. You see the Falls now and so, you might think, you could have seen them at any time. The thunderous spray and the colossal drape of water seem immemorial; but the scene is ceaselessly changing. The Falls drop into a chasm, the first gorge, running the whole width of the river. One third of the width out from the Zambia side there is an exit—the Boiling Pot Gorge, at right angles to the First Gorge, going a short way then turning at right angles to become the Second Gorge. In the elbow of the turn is the Boiling Pot, and so great a pour of water forced to such contortion gives ample reason for the name. The water churns in profound and frightful eddies, truly as if boiling, almost viscous.

The present line of the Falls is the most recent, one of eight previous lines that zig-zag downstream. The lines, zig or zag, go east-west, all connected by short more or less north-south ones. The Boiling Pot is the most recent. There is an explanation.

The Zambezi flows here in a bed of basalt of immense thickness —the depth cut in the making of the gorges is far from being the whole depth of the rock, probably another 1,000 feet. It was laid, as molten lava, by volcanic action of unimaginable immensity, and, slowly cooling, left a rocky sheet which covers great areas of Africa. As it cooled and shrank—as seems a reasonable guess— vertical fissures formed, some of which run in sets east-west, though others run in other main directions. But the east-west ones, again it may be guessed, were made more marked by subsequent movements of the crust. The very deep gullies so made became filled with softer material, almost clay-soft sometimes. The present line of the falls and the chasm into which they drop was one such gully. That is the clue to all else. From Katima Mulilo to the Livingstone area the river has been flowing in a more or less west-east direction but there it turns abruptly north-south for a distance. So doing it cuts across the lines of soft-filled fissures, making it possible for the river's force to cut out the soft filling—which it does with ease. It was so the first falls were made, seven away downstream from the present ones. Thereafter for a time there must have been an appearance of permanence (as there is now); but water never stops working.

The lip of that first fall was hard. Basalt is adamantine. But the river, prying and searching, must sooner or later have found a weak place; it must have dislodged a block of rock and, that done, pursued the advantage. The small lowering of the lip allowed more water to concentrate erosively, soon moving more blocks and, thus, bringing more concentration of erosion. The further that went the greater the multiplication of power drawn to it till the whole river's volume flowed to it, leaving the rest of the fall line. Then, not quickly but inevitably, a narrow gorge was cut back in a north-south direction till it reached another of the transverse east-west soft-filled lines. Then, relatively quickly, the soft material was gouged out and another falls line made

The process has continued and its seventh recurrence is the present Victoria Falls. The process still continues. Already there shows what, almost certainly, will be the next breach. Immediately above the Falls two lines of weakness, soft-filled fissures, cross the river. One, set back a little from the present lip, runs parallel with it from bank to bank. The other starts at Cataract Island, on the brink close to the west, or Rhodesian bank, and goes diagonally and rather upstream to the east, or Zambian, bank. At its start on Cataract Island the beginning is there; the river has cut a pronounced cleft. Later, when I flew over the Falls, I saw it clearly, and indeed the two lines of weakness.

Another Victoria Falls, above the present one, is on its way to being. Nor will it be the last. It will be repeated, or it seems it must, several times upstream until the point is reached where the river turns to a generally west-east course again. Then the water's power to cut will lose its advantage—the lines of weakness will cease to lie across the river's course. They will be more or less in the same direction as the flow.

Those are the geological facts. That is what made the Victoria Falls and will make new ones. But facts, however fascinating, leave much undeclared. After facts come other factors, atmosphere, character, emotional things. Enclosed by the spray in the bottom of the chasm I thought of Pluto and Persephone and making the ascent afterwards was like a return from the underworld.

The area of the Falls is really several worlds, close but irreconcilably different. You come up from the Plutonic plunge and there is the thunderous brink again, immense and miraculous, numbing the imagination but with nothing queer about it as there is in the abyss.

I went upstream, cruising for a few miles on a pleasure boat. So near the drama of the Falls there was an enormous peace. Passing from one wide placidity to another, hearing the sighing hippos, I found myself recalling the tranquillity of the upper

Thames. At early evening I sat on the riverside sward of a restaurant drinking beer. Monkeys swung in the boughs; the river, mirror-smooth, reflected the sunset. No great distance downstream the curtain of spray hung against the sky, and so near, the sound was peacefully softened.

Upstream and down there were other worlds. I went with Joe Susman and John Castle upstream to fish, clawing up rapids and subsequently shooting them to return. That was a world of labyrinths, all sorts of byways, tearing water and pond-smooth corners, woven through the forests of *matete* reed and papyrus.

I went downstream where the gorges, the other seven, are gouged into the plateau. There is a baobab tree, old and vast, said to be three thousand years old and looking no less, and in its boughs a viewing platform. From it you can see the pattern of the Falls' history. The harsh zig-zag of the gorges lies in a wide shallow valley and that, sun-blazed now, was once the river's course as it is now above the Falls.

You can walk to the dizzy brink and look down if you have the head for it. I found I had too little of the head for it. I looked, but with pangs. The drop is awful, so horridly precipitous. In the bottom there is the river, the mighty Zambezi, a thread. It twists and runs white and broken among the rocks that looks like gravel, monstrous though they really are. In the way of water seen from a height the action is stopped—waves on the sea seen from an aeroplane are stationary—so was the fume of the river, as if photographed.

Livingstone is a former African colonial town and utterly typical. It is also nothing but its highly individual self; and that, if contradictory, is true. In October and thereabouts it is also very hot indeed and, as I found it on first acquaintance, winsome. I have never ceased to find it so. It has a certain special character, hard to isolate. Its buildings are low and colonnaded, verandahed, deeply shaded. Main street, or, correctly, Musi-o-Tunya Road,

A gorge below the Victoria Falls

Johnny Uys and the author

is wide with the generosity of space that Africa can so well afford; the trees are tall, grouped graciously, often brilliant with blossom —jacaranda, flamboyant, and some others. Much of the whole place is embowered—bougainvillea, ipomoea, frangipani, poinsettia, cluster through everything. Round the corner and roundabout a little way there is the North Western Hotel and that is really the soul and spirit of the old style. A wide verandah runs the building's length and you go up wooden steps to sit in its wide shade for a beer. The hotel is ranged behind, on one floor, and enclosing a courtyard with a fountain and a tall canopied palm and shade heavy with the scent of frangipani.

The bar opens off the verandah and I met a queer man there. The heat was the cause. Darkness after a broiling day had brought no respite; there was a huge moist weight of heat, and the masochistic conventions of the old regime linger on—or at least did then. You must, said the notice by the door, wear a tie in the bar after seven o'clock. That was a severe price to pay for beer that, in those circumstances, you *must* have.

The bar counter is a horseshoe. We sat on high stools finding brief relief in the cold beer but losing it as quickly in the hot clutch of collar and tie. I tugged to loosen the cling and felt his eyes. He faced me across the horseshoe and, my eye caught, he half smiled and signalled—slip the knot of the tie down, undo the top button. It was a poignant relief and I was grateful.

But that was just a respite. The bar became insufferable and I took my beer to a table on the verandah. It was cooler there, the air less used. Then the man joined me, quietly and suddenly there, He sat down opposite me, put his arms on the table and leaned towards me. His eyes fixed mine and he said nothing. Then, quietly, meaningfully, he asked what I was doing in that area. Then he nodded slowly, making that significant. What did he do, I asked.

'I am a hunter.'

'Are you? What do you hunt?'

'I hunt men.'

'I see—you hunt men. May I ask what men?'

'I hunt communists.'

'Oh really—where?'

'I hunt communists in the Zambezi.'

I thought it was time to go. I do not remember how I extricated myself.

It was at Livingstone, and I think it was Stuart Campbell who told me, that I learnt of blackstone, which is a famous thing. It cures snake bite—or so I was assured, and I am not unready to believe it. What it is, how found and where, I have no idea and found nobody to tell me. It is small, shiny, black and slightly translucent. The wound of the bite should be made to bleed, then the blackstone applied and allowed to become stuck. It absorbs the poison. It is an old remedy and, formerly, there was only one proper way to clean the blackstone after use. It must be cleaned in the breast milk of a woman. Now, more prosaically, warm cow's milk is used, and instructions with the stone prescribe water. It seems a poor substitute.

It is as effective for the curing of septic wounds, blood poisoning, anything of that nature in the superficial layers. That suggests its use for snake bite must be immediate or not at all.

Stuart Campbell was a good guide to Livingstone. He knew all its useful intimacies; he could find you a blackstone or, I am sure, a good witch doctor or any of the less obvious things. He knew a good Indian faith healer and told me of that when I had a bad back, and we did go to the man's house. I felt sure he would have cured me if he had been in.

He had an apt way with words too. He told me of someone's dog, a mongrel creature. 'It's like a de-tribalized lavatory brush,' he said.

He had dogs, but of the superior kind. He and they and his

wife Joy lived by the Zambezi ten miles from Livingstone, up-stream at a place called Fairyland. His lawn went to the river's margin, which was delightful but seldom trim. Hippo invaded it too persistently. But for the bitch it would have been worse. She was infinitesimal; she may have been more than twelve inches long, but not by much, but she was capable. She saw off the hippo, driving them with her tiny furry back into the river.

A great occasion came to Livingstone while I was there. The Prime Minister of Jamaica was on a state visit to Zambia and he was coming to Livingstone, and, to welcome him, so was the President, the well-loved K.K., Kenneth Kaunda. The town was abuzz from first light, all the people holidayfied about the place in their brightest clothes and, long before the appointed time, the long road from the town to the airport was lined and noisy with the cheering and the children. The children were several deep, sitting and waiting under the jacarandas, delightful in their vivid school dresses.

At the airport the great throng was there from dawn, impatient under the sun that now, at mid-morning, was blistering. The women were in clean and brilliant head scarves and dresses slashed across with colour, the men gay and the children running on the parched grass. Everyone sang and the air hung still in the blaze of sun. Just occasionally warm wafts of air stirred through the leaves.

As is invariable upon such events, the arrival was late. But at last there was the aeroplane, and it landed, and there was the Prime Minister, not visible beyond the crowd, but his voice through the loudspeakers saying the things right for the occasion. He appealed to his African racial antecedents, stressing kinship, though, indeed, he was suavely trans-Atlantic.

Then there was the President, replying in his richly round voice, drawing fervent responses from the people. Then the children sang, the men beat drums and in all the fervour the President led the singing of a song I had not heard before, some sort of national song, perhaps a song of Independence; but anyway a deeply emotional link between the President and the people. First there was his strong voice, then the people, hanging upon his mood, responding. It was rather moving and very African.

The Prime Minister and the President came off the tarmac now, in procession through the terminal building to the cars. All was solemn and portentous but, because it was African, also a happy tropical festival and, for the people and the President, a communion. It was over, and going back into town, there were the children still under the jacarandas, ready to cheer anyone and ready to smile and laugh and make the jolly most of every moment. It had been a lovely sun-drenched exotic occasion.

16

I bypassed Kariba, the enormous man-made lake and the dam, and if that seems odd it was because my time had its limits and downstream, further east, there was more excitement than that offered—the country beyond Chirunda, the Zambezi Valley. It is uninhabited, untouched bush, with nothing of man but a Game Department camp, a safari camp, and a couple of airstrips. The Game Department camp, Mashika Camp, was to be my base. The three of us headed out from Lusaka late one morning.

I thought, and so did Kay, that we should be there comfortably before evening because it was no great distance, probably not more than a hundred miles, possibly less. But Smoke Tembo shook his head. 'About midnight we arrive I think.'

'About midnight—that short journey?'

'It is slow, last part.'

I was probably happier for not knowing then that that was, classically, a part of Smoke Tembo's low-toned understatement. Only time was to show what lay below his placid manner. How could I have known then that he was a witch doctor? I never did discover that until after we had parted. He was a snake doctor. There was Smoke, gentle mannered, a happily pleasant young man, respectably immaculate in his game guard's uniform. His khaki bush shirt and shorts were starched and shining from the pressing iron, his rifle oiled and clean, all about him parade-good to the last stitch. He was good looking too.

He drove the Land Rover and we did well and bravely for the

first part. The road was good, a modern one, wide and firm and breasting over the roll of the country in such fine style that we, Kay and I, could not understand why Smoke should have such pessimism. Past middle afternoon we stopped for a while, and Kay and I, the better for past experience, had a spirit stove which heated for us a tin of stewed steak. But canned stewed steak, luke-warm, finger-picked from the opened can, loses it small appeal quickly. I ate little. Smoke stood by passing the time and, about two hundred yards off, a cheetah sat watching us. That was all the visible life. The good broad road wound into both distances empty and unused and both sides of it the bush stretched endlessly under the sun. It was utterly still and quiet, the cheetah sat, and we drowsed a little.

We were unworried. The sun was still high, the road pencilled into the distance, we had still much of the day. We could see the mountains of the Zambezi Valley ahead of us. We sailed on down the good road with contentment and, soon, when Smoke Tembo said there were hot springs a little way off the road, we were careless enough of time to stop for that.

They were small springs, starting with a little pool, a yard or so across, and going down from there in falling runnels and pools and looking like any other upwelling of spring water apart from a faint drift of steam. The only clue on sight was the frogs, dead ones, bloated and floating. But why, I wondered, should frogs, in their own environment, have no premonitory sense of that danger? On the face of it the hot water was taking a steady toll. But is it possible to guess the working of all checks that keep the species in balance? There are a great many frogs in Africa; the total can well afford those few deaths in the hot water. It *was* hot, not scalding, but too uncomfortable for the fingers.

Then we left that fine and comfortable road. Smoke swung us off on to what would be called a dirt road, though this was more of rock, and treacherously uneven. We were coming into the

198

mountains and the road clung through pitching contours that tested the will of the Land Rover to claw its way. We were dropping off the high plateau, making the descent to the valley, feeling slowly down the wild escarpment. Smoke, always equable, persuaded the Land Rover like a pram.

We cleared the fall from the heights and in the valley had a better road, a quite good dirt road, and Kay and I, who had fallen to a rather distraught searching ahead for signs of a village, were glad. Through the careless hours of day thirst had accumulated. Now it tormented, and suppose there were no village ahead, no store, no beer. In spite of the sound road the miles rolled under us with no sign. But Smoke drove placidly, and when we did ask he said that soon, yes soon, there would be a store. There was at last, in a sparse little straggle of huts, rather forlorn and remotely alone. The store was shut and battened.

Smoke found the proprietor, who came with his key, and we were better after the beer. There was no more habitation, no more human life. We went apparently endlessly on. Darkness came and hours passed.

Then, startled from lethargy, we had stopped and were in a village. Someone was holding a paraffin lamp and the shallow light showed the people sitting before doorways and grouped politely round us. Children brought chairs, one for Kay and one for me, and a paraffin pressure lamp to hang on a bough.

The children clustered in the light, sitting in the deep dust. One, a girl about ten, smoothed the dust with the flat of her hand, then drew in it with her finger. She drew and they recognized. 'Larnd-roover,' they declared, and so it was. She smoothed and drew again. 'Moto-car,' they said. They made the appropriate noises.

I got down too, squatting in the dust. I drew funny faces and children of whatever colour have the same response to that. I drew animals—the first was an elephant—and they declaimed a word that, clearly, meant elephant. We did as well with giraffe, hippo, and lion.

I left them to their drawing, awaiting the return of Smoke Tembo. He had gone somewhere to fetch people who were to come on with us to Mashika Camp. He was a long time, or so it seemed, as if time had stopped.

The children chattered quietly and the adults in the half-shadows at the edge of the light murmured subduedly. We sat silently. It was a small human enclosure in darkness softly dense as a cushion; we were a weak cell of light. Beyond there was an immensity of darkness to anywhere else. The night sounds of the bush intensified the sense of isolation—as the sound of cicadas and frogs always does.

Smoke Tembo came back, with our passengers, women, one with a baby. The lost little village was the last habitation—I believe it was a Game Department one—beyond there was night-black uninhabited bush. Somewhere in it was Mashika Camp. Bearing round to reach the road our headlights swept the huts, picking up brief domestic flashes. The night was hot, too hot for confinement in the huts; children were put to sleep outside. Before one a woman sat; her five children were in a row in the dust, on their sides curled in sleep. The oldest might have been eight.

Then we left and the village was gone and had become unreal at once. There was nothing but the wild dark and the sharp swathe of the headlights. The 'road' was a directional guide rather than anything made, a passage forced by what had gone before, never level, pitching and pitted. Reaching growth scrubbed the Land Rover's sides and we lurched through, diverging for fallen trees, threading between rocks. Perhaps we averaged five or six miles an hour; it often seemed too fast.

We came to the first donga and I thought that even for a Land Rover it was not negotiable—not even, surely, in daylight. A donga is a rough channel, a bouldery trough that, at the height of the rains, rages with torrents going to the river. That leaves the rocky litter that most dongas have, and now they were dry. The drop into this one was loose and very steep.

Smoke, impassively, put us into four-wheel drive. We went over the brink. We pitched, and by sliding avoided the first boulder, then gripping again and seeming, as Land Rovers will, to walk down the drop, picking steps. I heard the shuffling tumble of the women in the back. We reached the bottom; Smoke put us to the climb. The engine screwed its note and, roaring and clawing, we began the clamber. We got halfway up.

Then the engine stalled; the lights went out. The blackness swept in. In the silence, suddenly and close, there was the coughing grunt of a creature. Smoke prodded at the starter.

The engine re-awoke, raced to a scream, and we plodded up the rubbly side and over the brink. We heard our passengers unravelling themselves.

There were many dongas. I lost count of them and of time. The bruising sequence was the same at each. In the interim we picked a slow way, weaving into the endless black, disturbing momentarily seen animals. A leanly speckled flash of creature leapt from the headlights, scrabbling in panic. 'Serval cat,' said Smoke because I asked. I am still sorry I did not ask again. An animal about the size of a fox, brilliantly black and white, with a heavy cape of white above its short legs, appeared and was gone. It looked like a zorilla or striped polecat very greatly enlarged. I think it was a honey badger.

Kay had become limply unexpectant of any end; I was not confident and even Smoke was wilting. But not much further he said and, about half an hour later, we stopped.

We were in a space, in a scatter of white-walled chalets. It was Mashika Camp and the women were climbing stiffly out and Smoke was sounding the horn. I guessed it to be about 1 a.m. A

man came soon, hurriedly dressed and still blinking. I was ravenous but he was pathetic and I told him no, don't bother now to
cook a meal—just give me a piece of bread to make do till morning. Then, safe under the mosquito net, I lay wakefully for a time
thinking of food and hearing the hippos outside mumbling
gutturally and scuffling their hides against the wall.

Sunrise came cheerfully, showing the spacy order of the camp.
The chalets, thatched and sound, stood apart and in the middle the
eating place, with a high pitch of thatch and open sides in the
nsaka fashion. A backwater lay below, a quite narrow gut of
water and beyond that an island some miles long and a mile across,
and beyond that again the distant shine of the main river. The
hippos of the night had come from that channel; now in the
growing day they were drowsing under the matted weed on
the surface. In some parts it blanketed the surface and, as I watched,
it heaved and lifted. A hippo's head, pink rimmed at eyes and
ears, came through. It sighed vastly, murmured enormously, and
sank again. Far across the island a party of elephant grazed.

The man of the night before had come up from behind—'Every
morning the elephant are there, and in the evening, you will see,
they will be here, just across the water. Every day the same—
I am William, William Manguwi—I am cook in this camp. You
want me to make breakfast?'

Kay had come now and was hungry too. But, we now learnt,
when you come to the camp you bring with you your food for
William to cook.

'I try to find an egg,' William said, and, when we had had that
the long hungry day stretched ahead of us with no promise of
more. You had to bring your own beer too, and now, still early,
it was 101 degrees Fahrenheit in the shade and getting hotter
and we had four bottles of beer to last till who could say when.
The tsetse flies had made a rampant start on the day.

The tsetse is master there—or tyrant. It dictates that this is un-

inhabited country. There had been people—the formidable Chikunda tribe and others—but the tsetse had forced them out. Cattle
cannot be kept in tsetse country but I could believe that tsetse
could force evacuation anyway. It can come near to making life
intolerable.

It is unimportant looking, rather bigger than a house fly and
quite similar. The main distinction is the wings, which fold one
over the other in the manner of scissors. But, undistinguished as
it is, recognition soon becomes instant—though, however quick,
usually too late to prevent biting. It seems slow, a rather clumsy
flier; but it is a rare and lucky swipe which swats it. In the interval
between its alighting on the person and the vengeful slap it will
have stabbed once, twice or thrice. Each stab can make a swelling
that may make difficult the bending of arm or leg. You may, in
any hour, acquire dozens of bites.

They give no peace and, in my experience, no repellent repels
them. Only the nightly retreat under the mosquito net gives
respite. They are, of course, bearers of sleeping sickness, or some
species are, and in cattle and horses they cause *nagana* which is
similar. Evidence suggests that cattle are more susceptible than
man—cattle cannot be kept in tsetse areas but man survives. They
made me desperate and distorted me, but I took no sickness.

But we were there and so were the tsetse, a fact to be lived
with—but what could we do about food? 'We hunt later?' asked
Smoke.

Yes, we would hunt; and, perhaps, we would find Johnny Uys.
They had told me about Johnny Uys at the Game Department,
as had others. He was almost legendary.

'Marvellous fellow, Johnny—a hunter you know, but an extraordinary naturalist too. Spent all his life in the bush, that's his
context, inseparable from the bush. A great chap on trees, though,
God knows, so he is on everything else in the bush. But particularly trees. He flies over the bush—he's a good pilot—and he spots

203

a tree that's different, different green or shape or texture, and he marks it. Then, later, comes walking to find it, and he knows his way in the bush like walking down a street. You won't find a tree he can't give the scientific name to and everything else about it, straight off.'

Johnny Uys was in the Zambezi Valley now, leading safaris, and, Smoke said, he had a camp in our vicinity.

Meanwhile I went alone out of the camp. The sun was high now and hot, a white pour of light and, again, I had the overwhelming sense of a burning of life in every inch. Something, I had no glimpse to know what, erupted from its camouflage at my knee and was gone. A few yards on a rustle through the yellow strew of stems showed the going away of a snake.

There was a confusion of evidences. Skeins of criss-crossed tracks twisted through the thorn tangles and, as always, ubiquitously, treads of elephant and their huge globular droppings. Litters of blanched and broken bones under the trees lay from old kills and, inevitably, the hyenas had been at them—halves of pelvis, cracked skulls, shattered gapes of ribs. What the lion leaves the hyena gnaws. The hyena's skull is a revelation, so big, bigger than a leopard's, so massively powerful, able to split the biggest bone.

There was the skull of a half-grown elephant, which I guess to be exceptional. Fully grown elephant are inviolate, too big for any menace and, I would have thought, too formidable a parental guard for danger to touch their young. But there was this one, and I suppose a lion had found its unguarded moment. Perhaps it happens oftener than I knew. The skull though immature was massy, but not enough to have withstood the hyena's gnaw.

In the skull of an elephant, close to the eye, there is said to be a gland which, once a year, secretes a fluid. Whatever its purpose, it is held to have a very potent magic and is eagerly sought. From it you must extract a substance that looks like a small piece of stick, which is powerful medicine, very strong in bringing evil to another person. The great nerve which runs down the tusk is no less potent. If it is extracted and an enemy induced to step over it he is by that made impotent. You bury the thing in front of his door.

I was glad that I had not brought my rifle. I came upon a herd of impala, so incomparably svelte and perfect, and, had I had it, I might have been prodded by our need for food. They were grazing, about a dozen, and a buck stood guard. I walked slowly towards them, not deviating, lessening the impression of movement, and so came to within a hundred yards. But they still stood, alert now but not alarmed as they should have been. They had a protective fear of predatory beasts but no saving fear of firearms that could, treacherously, hit them from a distance. Then I made an abrupt movement and raised my arm. The buck lifted its dilated eye and barked gruffly. The herd sprang away.

That cannot convey the superb and liquid movement. The creature is standing, apprehensive, high head poised, great eye rigid. With no preparatory crouch, no apparent setting of the muscle, it flows into a high arc that could clear the length of a large car. The motion looks slow, almost suspended, and the landing seems to be without impact.

In the afternoon we did hunt and, as the way is when the need is urgent, we looked particularly for guinea fowl. They abound and are good eating if hung, and are not too difficultly agile. We found them first idling in a dry river bed and within reach of an easy stalk through scrubby cover. As good as in the cook's hands I thought, and was astonished when no bird dropped to the shot. I think Smoke Tembo was too. But he was a polite man. We found them again in ten minutes. I missed again. My confidence fell as faint as we were becoming for want of a meal.

When we found a guinea fowl perched in the high crotch of a

tree I took the stalk down to thirty yards and shot the bird. I had saved the meal if not my confidence and then Smoke found a spoor, neat bifurcated prints.

'Wart hog,' he said.

Wart hog is good meat and we followed the spoor for most of a mile, till we found the animal in a clearing, a boar, a fine big beast. It showed a good target, a clear shoulder shot, and I should have taken that. But I suppose I was smarting. I would take a head shot and make a neat and instant kill. The wart hog ambled off when I fired. There was a long pause.

'You miss I think.'

'Miss a wart hog—that's not possible.'

Smoke said nothing; but I could see he had thought so too till now. Perhaps the guinea fowl I *had* shot had really died coincidentally of natural causes.

I made a target back at the camp. I scratched a ring on a tree and fired three rounds at it from about twenty yards. They made a half-inch group three or four inches to the left and up a bit from the bull. That deviation at twenty yards would be a wide miss indeed at eighty yards. In so much rough travelling the telescope sight must have been jarred from its zero-ing.

William cooked the bird for the evening. It was tough and very dry and, perhaps, was elderly. But theirs is an athletic life and our need allowed no time to hang the bird.

Next day in the afternoon I recalled the story of the meeting of Stanley and Livingstone. 'Johnny Uys I presume,' I was ready to say. We had come from the camp on, as it seemed to me, an inconsequential course, threading a few miles, crossing the dry river bed, then pitching down to reach the levels near the river. Then there was another Land Rover, coming up, and out stepped Johnny Uys, spare and fair and rather reserved. There, between the vehicles, in the bush, we shook hands, a bit awkwardly, a bit formally. I felt that in some way it was rather extraordinary.

'Well, mm, come to my camp—a bit down there, near the river.'

It was flat, under the trees, in a colonnade of the high white stems of the trees, with a spaciousness. The lofty canopy filtered the sun and in spite of the area the place had a cloistered feel. The tents, spruce and proper, were ranged neatly between the trees in a row and there was Glynne Uys coming hospitably out of one to ask if we would like coffee. The fly sheet made an overhang of awning in front, and we had the coffee there, very civilized and delightful in camp chairs.

The camp was temporary—the men were still working at the finishing of it—but it had an air of tranquil permanence, quiet and settled-seeming. Towards the further side the grass-fenced compound enclosed cooking quarters and such things, grass-thatched, and in the centre space the *nsaka* or eating place was prettily neat, oblong-round-ended, grass-thatched and grass-walled to hip height, open between.

Kay and I confessed our gratefulness for coffee; we admitted our food problem.

'Hungry?' Johnny said. 'Hungry? Hm, do something about that anyway.'

He went into the stores tent, next door, and from a big crate filled a box with canned foods.

'Keep you going for a time if you hunt a bit too.'

'But you don't know what hunger is—want to live through a famine to know that. But you see these trees—*Acacia alba?*'

They were the white-stemmed trees, silver white, patterned with dark seams. Their pods, yellowish-pink, curled and crumpled, like apple rings, strewed the ground.

'See the pods? Have dark brown beans in them—good to eat if they're cooked the right way. Need to be boiled three times—that makes them all right, but if you don't they can make you pretty ill.

'Well this time I'm telling you about there'd been a famine for some time. We, my men and I, hadn't eaten anything for nine days. Pretty desperate. Then the men started picking up pods of *Acacia alba* and opening them for the beans. "That's no good," I said to them, "much too slow. I know a quicker way," and I went down to the river where the elephant had been. They like the beans, you know, eat a lot of them—and you know how the stuff goes through them without being much digested? How their droppings are dry and loose when they've been lying for a bit? Well, I took some of them and rubbed them out in my hands—soon got a lot of beans while the men were picking for their few.

'Perhaps I was too anxious to eat, didn't cook them enough it may be. Anyway, I got food poisoning—very ill, vomiting, felt awful. But what made it worse was no one would come near me for days after. Every time I opened my mouth they said the stench of elephant droppings nearly knocked them over.'

We left Johnny and Glynne Uys and their shaded camp reluctantly, but with an invitation. The next night we were to go to dinner—there, in the empty bush, a dinner party. Two Americans —there to shoot film for television—would be there too. The intervening evening served for contrast; we had only the two bottles of beer left and our thirst was hardly to be borne. We sat with the bottles between us, pondering them.

'Shall we have one bottle now, shared between us—save the other for tomorrow, Kay?'

Kay stared at the bottle for thirty seconds. She raised her eyes to mine. She said nothing. I opened both bottles.

The fact that I remember little of the next day is I think akin to the failure in most cases to remember pain, something of mercy. Memory is blank for the hours between; it switches on to find us in the the Land Rover and on our way to dinner.

It was festive there with the party assembled and, though we

Buffalo skull,
near Mashika
Camp

*The Zambezi,
upstream of
Mashika Camp*

were, as we must be, in our same bush clothes, I think we felt as though dressed up, fine and formally, to go out. We had before dinner drinks, canned beer but, such refinement, poured in glasses. 'God, how good,' I said to Kay. She sighed and drank again.

In the *nsaka* a trestle table had been set and there were Johnny Uys and Glynne and, oddly suddenly present, another hunter, Mike Cameron, elongated and sinewy, six feet and some odd inches, and the two Americans. Johnny, as by a miracle, produced white wine, and under the thatch and under the hissing light of the paraffin pressure lamps, it was jolly at the table. Beyond, enclosing us, was the black unpopulated bush.

'The snakes will have moved into the thatch by now,' Glynne said, 'but I don't suppose they'll drop.'

'Hm, yes, snakes,' Johnny said, 'plenty here, various species—but mambas about the commonest—they talk of black mambas and green mambas. What I see here are all the same—a sort of grey-brown.

'They're no bother—it's the tsetse that's the bother. Drove out the original people here—that was the Chikunda—had to be moved out. They return as workers now, like some of ours here. They used to be warlike—soldiers and raiders—some of them had Portuguese blood in those earlier times. The Nsenga were the other people in the valley—Nsenga Luzi you know, the river area ones; there's a different Nsenga in the uplands—but anyway, the Nsenga were moved out too.'

The dinner was luxury, and restricted as the menu had to be, I remember it lovingly. There was guinea fowl, some sort of antelope meat, after that canned fruit and coffee.

'Hunting?' Mike Cameron was answering a question from one of the Americans—he shrugged—'I've no interest in shooting things—I do it—I'm a hunter. It's a job. I'm a professional.'

'Ha—reminds me,' Johnny said. 'In the old days, the colonial days, we used to get a particular sort of Englishman coming out from England to become D.O.s—members of the ruling class, the stuffy conventional sort. I remember one—got out here, very correct, very conventional. Soon after he decided to hunt—took his gun and went into the bush and, you know, he was completely new to it, never been in the bush before. Of course he got lost—walked and walked—no idea where he was. Night coming on. But then—stiff upper lip and all that—said to himself make the best of it—climb a tree, stay there for the night. And so he did.

'He was awakened in the morning by his servant—"Good morning, Bwana. Morning tea, Bwana"—the servant was a bit lower down the tree, coming up with the tray. If the bwana wants to spend the night in a tree instead of in the comfort of his quarters —well, he does.'

The talk turned to elephant.

'Did you know,' asked Johnny, 'that the lower jaw of an elephant makes the best lavatory seat you could possibly have? Better than anything devised by man.

'Very regular animals, elephant. Normally, except on overcast days, they start feeding at three o'clock, regular as clockwork, then they feed on, moving towards water, and feed on right through the night till eight o'clock next morning. Go to rest then. You'll see a bull lie right down, usually against an ant heap. But not a cow. In all my years in the bush I've never seen a cow elephant do that. She sleeps standing up.

'Antelope are the odd ones out in feeding pattern. Feed in the middle hours of the day, many of them, when it's hottest and most uncomfortable. It's an adaptation. Gives them immunity from lion. Then later, in the evening when the lion begin to move, they lie up. They've had plenty of time to adapt—hartebeeste, wildebeeste, kudu, all the different kinds of antelope—they've been here continuously for forty million years—the fossil record shows that. Seems a pity they're threatened now.'

That night, for the second successive night, there was a storm but a more blustering one, through the whole of darkness till, at dawn, it stopped abruptly. The storms were coming more often, the rains, so prematurely at the end of October, getting under way. It smelt wonderful in the morning, putting a bewitchment on the early air—the parched and gasping valley, or so it had been, taking a deep new breath. In many countries air can smell exquisite after rain and do so differently. Here it had a heavy freshness, if that may be said, spicy.

Soon after the time of sunrise, though, this morning, it was overcast, a pack of wild dog passed near the camp. 'I remember,' Kay said, 'my mother talking to me about wild dog.

'I was not to go to a particular place, she told me, because there were wild dogs there—she always warned me very seriously against wild dogs. But, all the same, I did go, and sure enough there was a pack and they had a kill. I knew I ought not to stay, and I think I was frightened, but I was fascinated. It was queer the way they fed. They would take a bite, ripping it from the kill, chew it, then rub their muzzles in the dirt and grass, come up with their muzzles plastered with it, then take another bite—and so on, each time the same.'

'And did your mother know where you'd been when you got back?'

'Oh yes—I had to confess—I had a good hiding. My mother told me angrily how silly I'd been—hadn't she always told me that wild dogs are very very dangerous, one of the most dangerous animals in the bush?'

We went hunting again, Smoke and I, anxious to get a wart hog but ready to accept anything that would stave off hunger. We walked a long way, Smoke tracking, reading the spoor, I with him with half my eye but seeing much else with the other half. It was in a way frustrating—Smoke was like a dog with its nose to a scent, head down, loping, losing it, casting, then finding it again, not stopping. I had to go with him, but, by the way, seeing so much that I would have liked to examine. There was a creature that abounded—an insect perhaps—I had no chance to see—about an inch to an inch and a quarter long, brilliant flame colour and with a sheen, like chenille. They were everywhere, and then there was a sausage tree, *Kigelia pinnata*, that odd but lovely tree with beneath it still, though rather late for that, a carpet of its great deep and luscious crimson flowers. And, once, briefly sweeping, a martial eagle.

But I could stop for nothing. We went on, stopping only occasionally for the loss of a spoor or its complicated doubling, then on again and I marvelling as often before at the nearly uncanny sense of direction an African guide may have. We walked many miles, not consecutively but this way and that way to the erratic turning of the spoor, weaving a pattern of miles till I was utterly disorientated. Smoke, through all, knew where we were.

We saw the quarry; he drew us on with distant sightings but we failed continuously to reach the chance of a shot. When, once, we did come within shot it was a female with young.

In the confusion of tracks—so multiple that it seems odd that sightings of animals are as few as they are—track over track making much of it unreadable, here and there were sudden startlingly clear prints, like signatures. Zebra I recognized, various antelope, and then obviously, clear and defined, the tread of a big cat.

'Lion,' said Smoke.

It was, in terms of meat won, hunger prevented, a failed morning but not utterly the worse for that. The rains had brought their change; the moistened air, no longer aridly scentless, was aromatic with hauntingly unidentifiable scents.

In one much trodden place there was a burrow, cavernous, like a vast rabbit hole. A wart hog burrow Smoke said and, big as it was, I wondered how the hunched up bulk of the shouldery beast could go in there.

'They go in backwards—for safety you see, so that a lion or leopard can't attack them from behind.'

'But how can they dig the great hole? How do they manage with their small cloven hoofs?'

'Well, they don't—they take over the burrow of an aardvark and change it a bit to suit themselves.'

I saw a tortoise, apparently the same familiar species sold in European pet shops, treading its sedate way over the game tracks. Smoke said nothing when I pointed it out. He picked it up with an inward air and, very carefully, put it in his pocket. He was quite evidently, and rather mysteriously, gratified, and I supposed that tortoise must be a specially valued meat. Later, having learned of Smoke's witch doctoring, I wondered.

It was after the end of my expedition that they told me.

'You should see him,' they said, 'handling the most dangerous snakes—mambas, cobras—picking them up, popping them in a sack, just nonchalantly, and, queer thing, he never gets bitten.'

I had to return, a year later, for a second expedition, with the Game Department's promise that I could again have the good Smoke Tembo. But, alas, there was no Smoke Tembo for me. He was in hospital.

'He came in in a pretty bad way, very ill indeed, vomiting blood—all the signs of snake bite. But he wouldn't say anything, wouldn't give a clue as to what had happened to him. His pride you know—should think that was more wounded than his body.'

On that return I came again to Mashika Camp but, this time, with John Kabemba. I came, rather more than for any other reason, because I wanted, particularly, to catch a vundu. The Zambezi Valley has quite a fame for vundu. The vundu is a fish, not by average standards a pretty fish. It is a catfish, and they, as a kind generally, tend to repel rather than fascinate and among them the vundu is monstrous. It grows huge, it is darkly heavily mucously brown and its tiny eyes are set in a great blank width of countenance extravagantly appended with very long barbules. It is also astonishingly powerful, by common report so powerful that it will snap like rotten cotton a line of eighty pounds breaking strain. I had heard too of the preposterously long initial run it made on being hooked. All this, and its special association with some of the most wildly remote places, had given it, for me, an aura.

William Manguwi came with us to be our guide when, walking smartly in the sweating heat, we left the camp and went the few miles to where, downstream of the big island, the whole splendour of the river's width faced us. It was wider there than above the Victoria Falls, not less than a mile and a half, a flat shimmer nearly, as it seemed, to the eye's reach. About three hundred yards out, by a long sand spit from the island, a party of hippo wallowed in gargantuan peace.

Their sighs and blowings and mumblings softened by distance, the distant cry of a fish eagle, enhanced the not truly describable sense of loneliness. I felt, not in any forlorn way, a sense of ultimate lostness—final wilderness.

That added to zest, further prompted by heavy swirls in the river. We were by a great still layby from the main stream, in the downstream shelter of the island. Fishing for vundu is without any delicacies but I, against advice, was not using a line of ponderous strength, one of twenty-five pounds breaking strain instead of the recommended eighty. But, as advised, I used a sizeable piece of meat for bait.

Its casting into the water was met immediately by a responsive swirl, a fierce wrench and all was slack. It was easy to diagnose. Tiger fish were there. The great swirls were theirs. One had taken the bait, bitten through the nylon line, robbed me of the hook; I had only two others, and, soon, they had been taken too. There was I, by the river, the river full of vast vundu, my last hook gone. I had given them too freely to people by the river.

'Perhaps you have another hook, any sort of hook,' John said.

'Look—see what there is.'

I looked without real hope. I need a strong hook and I needed wire to resist tiger teeth. I found just a very little spoon bait with a little, rather fragile, gold treble hook. It was attached to a fine wire trace, seven pounds breaking strain.

'You will try that?'

'Well—I suppose I can only lose it—but you know, John— *vundu*, on that!'

I squeezed on as big a piece of meat as the tiny hook would take, with the spoon blade flapping round it. It lacked the weight to be cast far; only about fifteen feet from the bank it sank. It lay for, perhaps, three minutes.

Then the line began to go and, gently for fear of the wire's fragility, I struck, set the hook; the line poured away as if it had taken life of its own. It ran and ran, a V-furrow in the surface showed the running of the fish, and the distance lengthened unbelievably. The fish came to where the hippo lay and, looking at the reel which had over three hundred yards of line, I saw that most was gone. The fish stopped then.

Could I then entertain just the smallest hope of catching it? I had felt the weight, the really quite queer power of the fish. But, didn't its reputation say, let it have its first run right out and it's finished—it squanders all it has on that first fantasy of running. Gently, tentatively, I felt through to the fish, bent the rod a little against its weight and, astonishingly, it yielded. It began to come.

'I might, I just might, get it, John—d'you know how to use a gaff?'

'What's that?'

'On the bank there, with the hook at the top. When I bring the fish right up to the bank—*if* I do—the gaff hook has to be pulled into its back—just firmly pulled in, not slashed, so that it can be pulled from the water—the line's not strong enough to pull it ashore.'

John picked up the gaff. He squared his weighty shoulders. A gleam had come to his eye. I was apprehensive. Wild use of a gaff loses fish easily.

Foot by foot, uneasily, sensitively, I brought the fish towards the bank—it was true then, what was said—the fish had made that first astounding run and, so it did seem, burnt its last flicker of energy. Then I saw it, coming inert, through the water, the broad blank spread of face, well over a foot of width. I looked at John. He was poised. His head was purposefully forward, barrel chest out; he gripped the gaff with both hands.

'Fingers crossed,' I said to myself.

I brought the fish to the bank. In a moment's glimpse I saw John with the gaff swung high. He brought it down in a hissing arc. It made deep purchase on the fish and, almost in the moment, he had dragged its huge flapping sepia bulk to the bank. It had been unconventional, but it had been effective.

'My friend,' said John, his hand on my shoulder, 'you must strike hard to get such a fish on the bank.'

Well—there it was. What more could be said? It weighed seventy pounds.

It was the evening of that same day that the insects came. Why, just that evening, I do not know. Any evening the light of the lamp in the *nsaka* would bring insects as light will, anywhere. But not as they came that evening, not in the nearly solid density of that invasion. There were many kinds of insects, and without the cicadas it would have been extraordinary, but not before or since have I seen cicadas swarm thus. They are big insects, an inch and a half long, hornily blunt and hard; they came in a swarm so dense that there seemed no space between them. They collided, one with the other and with everything else, with resounding impact, bashing us, settling in a seething pile on everything. The scrabbling thousands filled the air, covered every surface.

I found them a nuisance, a sort of plague; John found a large jar. He scooped up the cicadas, grabbed handfuls from the air, filled his jar and found another one.

'Bernard my friend, I take these home. They are a very good dish. We strip off their wings and fry them—it's a traditional dish—like locusts you know—those too, very good fried.'

William Manguwi was collecting also—'And ants,' he said. 'Earlier in the year I collect those. The white ants, and big winged ones when they hatch in big swarms. Take the wings off and fry them and they are very good too.'

'We shall not need the witch doctor,' he added as the rain began again.

'Why? Would you have needed the witch doctor if it hadn't rained?'

'Well—not really now, with the rainy season started, but sometimes when rain will not come and there may be hunger, then the witch doctor comes.'

He told me how the witch doctor made his medicine, very detailed and mysterious. I would have learnt more if I could have understood more. William's English was patchy. I did learn that the witch doctor spread a black cloth over the ground and above that made complicated medicine.

'And,' said William, 'the next day the rain comes.

'Or that is how it used to be—then the witch doctors were true, really true. Now they are not properly true. Their medicine is not as good.'

'Are there women witch doctors too?'

'Oh yes—a woman doctor will make medicine for a woman who is ill. But always she insists that the husband must not be in the house. If he is it will spoil the medicine.'

'What about snake bite? Can the witch doctor treat that?'

Yes, John Kabemba said, for a treatment he had seen you should pick up the victim to carry on your back and *you* should eat a porridge into which had been mixed a medicine given by the witch doctor. Then, soon, as you carry the victim, he begins to vomit—he vomits and vomits and vomits—that cleanses his system and he lives.

'I have seen many men who have had snake bite,' William said. 'There is a snake—a *malala*—and it is white and it is big. When it strikes it stands right up and strikes on top of the head. There was a white hunter who was attacked like that. He died in a few minutes.

'There was another white man who was here and he was a great snake man. He collected them. Once he picked up a puff adder but I think he did not hold it close enough to the head. It bent back and bit him. It took five hours to get him to Lusaka to be treated—but he did live.'

I have never learnt what snake William's *malala* was. A big albino cobra perhaps? I should have asked Johnny Uys.

We were walking the bush next day, he and I, because we needed a guinea fowl. We came upon a procession of Matabele ants.

'If you are going out to find honey,' William said, 'or to hunt, if you meet these ants you must look well at them. If they carry nothing in their mouths, you go home—it is no good—you will get nothing. But if they *are* carrying something in their mouths it will be good—you will get everything that you want.'

He stopped to pick two well-matched stones. 'Our matches,' he said, and put them in his pocket.

But all that was a year later. Now we, Kay and I, went with Glynne and Johnny Uys from their camp by the river to the permanent camp, near the river too, but closer to the hanging height of the escarpment. Johnny talked as we went.

'That thickety growth, see it? Right over, spreading—it's

218

Combretum mozambiensis—become a damn pest. Encroaching seriously. It forms thickets impassable to anything except elephant. Sometimes get up to twenty square miles of it in a unit. Not a lot of use either—rarely eaten by elephant, which would keep it down. Rhino and kudu like it though—kudu like the seeds. Local name's *jesi*—really just the Tonga word for "thicket".'

Later, lurching down a rugged slope, the reaching pod-hung twigs of a shrub scraped the Land Rover.

'That's a *Strophanthus* species—has a very rare form of seed dispersal. The pod opens, seeds come out, and they open a parachute, drift away on the wind.

'Useful, those seeds. They get a poison from them, use it on heads of arrows. But they use it as well for women who have trouble with childbirth. They make a paste from the seeds and put it in a cut made in the woman's arm. Then, as they say, the baby just walks out.'

There was a tree, felled and three parts burnt, leaving a copious and very soft white ash.

'*Combretum imberbe*—they burn it like that to get the ash. Use it as a pigment for painting the face and body for rituals.'

We paused for a time when we came to the other airstrip and, browsing round, I fell to watching a colony of termites. The entrance to the nest was there, a hole in the ground. They create a faint uneasiness, these feverish insects—they have too sharp a suggestion of a hyper-systematized industrial society. They are too exclusively deployed, hurrying ceaselessly, all converging on the entrance with no thought or moment for anything but that. They severed blades of dead grass, then carried the idiotically disproportionate burden, several inches long, tilting it up in front or backing with it, all in a frenzy of industrious duty.

Johnny looked over my shoulder.

'They take the grass into the nest and chew it up, make a sort of mush of it and spit that over the walls of the nest. It grows a mould, and the young feed on it. Guinea fowl join up the life cycle—they eat the termites and the result is that the eggs spend a period in the intestine of the bird, finally being ejected in the excrement.

'There's another sort of termite—the ones which inhabit the huge heaps—and if you knock the top off the heap and sprinkle water on it, it suggests the sort of humidity that they respond to. They begin to flight. Then you build a fire on the downwind side of the heap. They come, wind-borne, over the fire, it burns their wings and they drop. Then you collect them and cook them. Very good eating they are; the Africans love them. They taste like bacon, very full of fat.'

The camp was a few hundred yards up from the marshy margin of the river, where the land climbed in a series of rises to the sheer of the escarpment. The little cluster, a circular *nsaka*, a hut or two, the grass-roofed stores, lay in the broken shade of a big acacia. It was midday or thereabouts, very hot, and there was beer in the stores. We were taking that gratefully when I saw a tiny frog. It had come under the grass wall and was by my feet, apparently swollen with the pompous pride that small and chubby men may sometimes have, preposterously puffed up almost to bursting and erected on to the very tips of its toes. I stooped to look at it, and it strove to greater size.

'It's a *Breviceps* species,' Johnny said. 'Funny little thing, isn't it, not much in the way of defences, and honey badgers love it—never miss a chance to eat it. So this is what it does—inflates, blows itself right up and walks on the tips of its toes—tries to give an impression of being quite big really and not too easy to gobble up.'

There were pieces of rock in the camp, arranged in a sort of display before a hut, some with shining glances of mica, others with metallic sparkles.

'From a place about ten miles from here—remarkable place—

you'd never know about it if you weren't told, too deeply lost in the bush. But there it is, a small hill—just a great heap of minerals, never seen anything like it elsewhere. The soil's eroded away and left the stuff underneath, and that happens to be this intense concentration of minerals—a lot of mica there but all sorts of other things too, crystals of many sorts including topaz, and certainly, if you looked long and hard enough and, I suppose, with knowledge enough, you'd find diamonds and probably gold too. Anyway, it's a fascinating place—like to go there? All right—I'll tell Smoke Tembo how to go. Will you go tomorrow?'

Now we had to start our return. Night would drop soon after six, and we were going by river, something best done by light of day. The boat lay in a small inlet and, Johnny said, it, and the outboard engine, had been submerged for a period. This was to be its first outing since drying out and cleaning.

'Hope it's all right,' Johnny said.

'And with that small doubt in our minds we'll set off down this great croc-infested river,' Glynne added.

Without too much reluctance the engine came to life. We pushed off. As we swung into the current the engine faltered, then stopped. Johnny attacked it with compressed fury; I think he must have striven with it before. Then it started again, became steady, gained confidence, and we turned down-river. A man from the camp had come with us as pilot because the river is treacherous. He was little, with a face like a shrivelled black apple, his body stringily knotted with muscle.

He stood, hand on the tiller, eyes anxiously straining ahead, behind him the panorama dropping astern. At first the mountains were near, rugged upthrusts close with bush to the summits. Then they stood back with the widening valley till the huge cloud-piled sky filled in, with the broad plane of river below and the mountains low on the horizon. We tacked and quartered, this way and that, finding the channel, mile after mile of sky-drenched vista falling away over our wake, with no sign of man or anything else to break the serenity.

At last when signs of evening were beginning to shade the sky, the long island was on our beam and, somewhere beyond, lay Johnny's camp and ours. We began a last long diagonal, crossing to come downstream of the island to turn under it. So the channel went, and when we saw the hippo we had a quarter of a mile still to go.

We saw the hippo distantly, its white bow-wave first. It was apparent almost at once that it had seen us. Its speed was extraordinary. Its course, arrow straight, was set for interception. We accelerated, pushed the outboard to its highest whining pitch. We gained no advantage. The hippo's bow-wave stood higher and now very rapidly closer. Its course and ours seemed certain to meet. I could see its pink rimmed eyes now and I thought they looked angry. We were braced; only feet now between hippo and us. We cleared, we just passed the hippo. Its line crossed ours just aft of us.

Perhaps that panic crescendo of speed was too great a strain. We rounded the lee of the island and the engine stopped. We floated idly, the island to one side, the mainland to the other. Evening was imminent. Johnny strove with the engine, swore at it with husky passion.

'Come on, Bernard—give it a bloody pull when I say—now—pull—again, now—pull.'

He tinkered, I pulled. The engine slept. We paddled the man ashore to walk to camp to bring help, but that was likely to take a long time. It was a long walk. The light was dimming.

'Well,' said Glynne, 'here we are, in the heart of Darkest Africa, night coming on apace, benighted in a small boat on the great wild Zambezi, the place seething with hippo and croc. They'll all be out soon. Resent us I expect. Ah-hm.'

Johnny swore and fiddled. I pulled as directed. The engine gave no suggestion of life. Not for a long time. Then for one pull no different from the others it surged into full life. In some way unrevealed to me, who am no mechanic, Johnny must have touched the appropriate chord. We reached Mashika Camp as the curtain of darkness touched down.

Next day Johnny instructed Smoke Tembo with care, and his directions must have been minutely precise. We threaded the bush with apparent exactitude, and I not able to detect what were the directive markers. We went, as I could tell, from point to point, but it was all anonymity to me. Wild and tangled anonymity, lonelier than I thought anywhere could be. Then where large stones littered the ground Smoke said that by a particular stone we had to turn. Of those utterly similar stones one was *the* stone. We turned, soon after we stopped.

'We walk now,' said Smoke.

We walked, going slowly for the roughness of the country, wild stony hills openly forested, foothills to the mountainous upsweep to the escarpment. I saw no way, had no sense of differences this way or that directionally significant. Each of the hills, quite low, not unlike the repetitive not large hills of Devon, though these were jungle-wild, matched its partners. Smoke went ahead purposefully and, as it seemed, with certainty. We climbed one hill after another, then on one he stopped.

'We have reached it. We are there.'

The ground was rough, jaggedly stony, randomly heaped; though no soil lay, a few scrawny trees had rooting. The stones shone with coloured gleams and glinting veins; it was rather as if a huge mineralogical museum had tipped its contents there.

'Bring me back a nice diamond,' Glynne had said, 'one about the size of the Koh-i-Noor,' and scanning that careless treasury, it did not seem completely unlikely.

We made our clawing search as well as we could, with time

nodding at our elbow, Kay and I feverishly turning through the stones.

'Look,' Smoke said. On the ground lay the broken parts of an entire bole of a tree, fossilized where it fell, turned crystalline now, all the grain, the knots, the natural form, expressed in gemmed sparkle.

'I think we go now,' Smoke said soon. 'It is a long way back—we have to go slowly.'

We had found no diamonds, no emeralds, no topaz and if we had we might not have recognized them. But we left burdened, struggling back with a weight of pieces—I with some of the tree that, who knows how long before, had borne leaves there. I hung back, letting the others draw ahead so that I could the better feel the primitive loneliness of the place.

17

I left the valley because Feira lay ahead and Feira was my journey's end. Going that way, eastwards with the river, you come out of the wildly broken country held between the escarpment and the river and, with the heights falling back, are in a lower rolling area. It is rugged still, with some sparse habitation, and still its recurrent dramas of landscape. Not far from Feira, a part made uneventful by the map, there is the Mpata Gorge; the river is constricted in a defile of stygian grandeur, for all the sun's brilliance.

At last there is Feira, an outpost, unmistakably something of finality, held in the cleft of the Zambezi, mighty here, and the Luangwa River, a fine stream too which empties from the north into the parent river. On the distant southern bank of the Zambezi there is Rhodesia, across the Luangwa there is Zumbo in Mozambique.

I went to the Boma, as is the way, and it lay in the shade of an enormous baobab tree with a bole not less than twenty-five feet in diameter and hollow. 'Many snakes in there,' someone said, and such old hulks can give harbourage to cobras. That was the last baobab in Zambia and it could be as good a totem as any at that final place because no other tree is more involved with the sense and life of the country. Few other trees can have lived as long there, probably none other. Its life span can be three thousand years and for much of that time it will have given various uses to the succession of generations—often of one family, because a

225   Z–P

family may have a hereditary right in one tree. Beneath its slightly satiny but rather metallic grey bark there are fibres which make rope; its seeds are used as an antidote to *Strophanthus* poisoning; its fruit pulp is a rare rich source of vitamin C; its seeds are edible and its young leaves are cooked and eaten; all its parts have their uses in traditional medicines. Additionally there are the bees which colonize it, making their enormous honeycombs within and without. Not surprisingly, in some tribal cultures it is worshipped as a fertility symbol. Any baobab not in uninhabited country has its oddity made more odd by the recurrent sutures up its vast bole, the healed scars of old climbing places. The final oddity of the tree, so great in its bulk of bole and its tentacle sprouting of boughs above, so anciently old, is that at last it dies suddenly, rots and falls away, leaving nothing but a quite small declivity.

The D.S. was in the Boma, with his assistant and the higher police officers of the area and, as I had so often found elsewhere, they were politely and warmly welcoming, gentle mannered. The assistant D.S. took me to the rest house. It was above the river, on a lifting rise; its verandah commanded a view over this ultimate soil of Zambia to the river's wide breast of water beyond. There seemed to be a quietness, but that was not really an absence of assertive sound but, again, the queer air that frontier places have. It may be that the consciousness of that is greater when the frontier is a tangible barrier of water, and this was a very great one and, beyond, not one foreign country but two. I thought of that first frontier where I had seen the minute and infant river rising in the roots of a tree fifty yards from the Congo frontier. That had had a strange air too. Now here was this frontier where I was to leave the river I had followed so far. I saw its shining distances, so huge, receding remotely. Blue mountains lay beyond.

Under the steep fall of the bank, by the river, women were washing clothes and fetching water, standing to their knees in the river.

'It is worrying, that they do that.' The assistant D.S. shook his head. 'There are many crocodile in the river—but they do it, you cannot stop them.'

Those who fetched water trod slowly up the thirty or forty feet from the river, erect, not spilling a drop from the big vessels on their heads.

The assistant D.S. left, and, for a while, I watched a procession of Matabele ants which, as usual, seemed endless. But then this one did end. The moving black strip passed on and there, behind, was one more ant, out of touch. It was overwhelmed with obvious panic, bereft of its corporate being, fallen into a calamity of personal responsibility. I cajoled it on to a piece of stick and transferred it to the tail of the procession. In the instant it hitched on, scrabbling back into anonymity.

In the heat of afternoon I walked out of Feira, climbing away into the bush behind, facing back into Zambia. The whole horizon north of the river was filled with a crenellation of bluebell-coloured mountains. They looked inviolable, as if they would mark the end of all journeyings, and I recalled with a sense of strangeness all the places, all the people, all the hours of day and night that I had known on the other side. Could they still be there, the mission at Chavuma, the club and the people at Balovale, lovable Senanga?

The road, if such it must be called, so humped with rocks, so devious among the erratic contours, was ruddy with the eroded dust of old rocks, nearly pink. The sun blazed back from the tiny shattered crystal of the dust. Inevitably there was a baobab beside the way, a stripling by the standard of that by the Boma, with a bole probably only twelve feet in diameter. Its great white blossoms were littered under it.

Then there was a village and, unless memory is utterly false, its name was Chindada, just a little straggle of perhaps a dozen huts. The dogs ran out, making a fury of teeth and snarling, and I thought I was to be mauled. But the men came, ordered the dogs

227

back and were polite, greeting me smilingly and, I am sure, wishing me well, though they and I had not a word of language in common.

I had to turn back in the end because the sky began to take its evening colour and this was not good country to walk in darkness and alone.

That evening at the rest house when candles were lit and the beer bottles opened, there was company. I think the assistant D.S., who was there too, had arranged it. Our guests, old men, were from outside Feira. Kuyeli Kanjagwali Malunga was seventy-five and from Chindada as, I think, was Moses Zeoya Chendiende, and he was certainly little younger.

With the beer they grew loquacious, very willing to meet my wish for comparisons—how, I was wondering, did their customs, Chikunda ones, compare with those of the far-away Ndembu of the source country. A girl's puberty rituals, one of the most fundamental, were they similar? Not dissimilar it seemed, though I found it hard to follow all the softly mumbled words. Certainly the girl was confined with her instructress, kept in a hut for two weeks with her—or so she was if the food lasted. Sometimes it did not. If at one week's ending there was no more for the instructress, the one week was thought acceptable.

They rambled on, drifting through old memories, explaining customs, telling of past prowesses. Great hunters they had been, in the particular manner of their people, driving the game, catching it with nets and spears. Each man owned a net though all were used connected, and the practice was whichever net ensnared the animal, its owner must be the killer. But, no more, they said, all that has gone.

But not all was past. The witch doctor still plies his arts, and particularly in cases of *impondolo*, which is possession by a spirit. He would come and, with his subject, lie on the floor of an open-sided shelter. There he would lie, communing with the *impondolo*, till about four o'clock in the morning; then, calling the relatives, he would tell them of the medicines to be prepared and used.

But the witch doctor was also the source of *lukanko*, and that was pretty important in social life. It is a medicine, they told me, prepared by the witch doctor and which you must give to your wife, but without her knowledge. If then she goes with another man he will become ill. He will have very severe burning headaches and terrible disorders of the stomach and with a great swelling of the stomach and legs. So he will be for two or three weeks. Then he will die.

But there is an antidote and that too you may have from the witch doctor. It is much used. Many men get both—the one to give to their wives, the other to protect themselves.

'And the wife,' I asked, 'does she know nothing of this?'

'A woman will not know anything at all about it—not until a man she has had dies.'

I told them of the forms of greeting and respect I had seen in other places—how the Lunda and Luvale peoples will clap softly and stoop their knees, that and other forms elsewhere.

'Here we have *kukenga*,' one of them said, 'that is for men,' and, demonstrating, he stood making a backward and forward alternate shuffle of the feet.

'Men do that. Women bend their knees three times.'

It was next morning that I met Simon Ngulolube. I had gone with the assistant D.S. through country to the back of Feira and we came upon Simon working his plot of land. His wife, seventy or thereabouts, was naked above the waist. Not hurriedly, with dignity, she raised her garment to cover her withered breasts. That she should feel so impelled made me, as a white man, feel a corporate shame. Simon Ngulolube was more than eighty, tall, still straight, slow, but lean and strong. He was of the Nsenga people and, in former times, before the tsetse had forced evacuation, had lived in the Zambezi Valley.

He had been a fisherman and a subsistence farmer and, often, a hunter. Now, living out his old age in Kamwangala village, he worked his land day by day; but I think he found a greater, and sad, reality in his dreams of things gone.

'Life was better there, always plenty of food even if there was little rain. We had our traditional life and now when I am old I am sad for it. That was my home. There I had my wives and my nine children, and our life was good. We ate fish and sweet potatoes, bananas, beans, cassava, ground nuts and tomatoes, the meat of game, pawpaw and mango. It was good and we were not often ill.'

'And when you were ill?'

'Small illnesses we cured ourselves—with herbs and roots and such things. For bigger illnesses we had the witch doctor.'

I asked him, as I had those at Feira, what in the way of his tribe was the form of greeting.

'For a great chief we sit on the ground and slap the right thigh with a soft hand.'

'But for ordinary people?'

'For them we clap our hands quietly.'

A few miles distant, in a village the name of which I forget, I had the chance to use that first greeting but did not. I met Chief Mkolikola Mbolama, a man of the Nsenga too. I think he was tolerant. I do remember also that among the playing children was an albino, completely without black pigmentation. In his form— hair, features—he was as African as the others, but the tight close-curled hair of his head was palest flaxen, his skin delicately, almost transparently fair, not sun-tanned. His eyes, pink, were perpetually screwed with a failure to face the brilliance of the light. He gave me a pathetic impression of a degree of rejection among the others, but I expect I imagined that. I have, since then, seen other African albinos.

It was the following day, that at last I walked from the rest house, past the grass-walled market place, under the heavy arch of trees and out to the final tip of land, a point caught between the Zambezi's huge width and the inflowing Luangwa. This was the last bit of Zambia, its final feet. There, as tranquil and as quietly set as they may be found across the world, were anglers. They stirred from their placid depth to greet me quietly, making room on the shelving bank worn by the sitting of many such sessions.

All had their lines out. Their rods were pliant sticks, pressed vertically into the ground and arched into a bow by the pull of lines tight to where their lead-weighted hooks lay on the bottom far out. At each rod's tip was a bell. You must, they explained, cast your tackle far into the heavy flow of the Zambezi, letting the flow carry it round and draw out more line until it came to rest a long way out in the mingling of the two rivers. That was the best place.

'What do you expect to catch there, vundu?'

'Yes, vundu, and perhaps a tiger fish.'

'And what bait do you use?'

'Usually it is a piece of meat, but sometimes it is a piece of fish.'

I had brought my tackle and, as I set it up, they inspected it with slow gravity, nodding, fingering rod and reel and exclaiming with pleasure at the hooks. They pointed for me just where I should cast for the greatest advantage of the current and, when I had cast and my bait's position had their approval, we sat peacefully. I gave them the last of my hooks, we shared beer, and the quiet hours passed until it was evening. It was my journey's end.

Index